A NEW DEVELOPMENT STRATEGY

A NEW DEVELOPMENT STRATEGY

ROBERT J. ALEXANDER

ORBIS BOOKS
MARYKNOLL, NEW YORK

To Ted de Bary

CONTENTS

Preface   ix

Introduction   3

1   Alternative Development Strategies   19

2   The Import Substitution Strategy   31

3   Prerequisites for Import Substitution Strategy of Development   47

4   Development Priorities in the Import Substitution Period   71

5   The Post-Import Substitution Crisis   93

6   New Export Possibilities in the Post-Import Substitution Period   127

7   Some Latin American Examples   139

Postscript   157

Bibliographical Note   167

Preface

This book is the result of a quarter century of observing and studying the process of economic development in Latin America and Spain and of reading extensively about its progress elsewhere. In an earlier volume, published more than decade ago, I tried to sum up many of my ideas on the subject at that time.

The line of inquiry put forward in the present book evolved in the process of researching and writing a study of the political and economic development of Brazil between 1930 and 1967. As my studies for that work progressed, I was struck with the importance which import substitution had had in the industrialization of Brazil, and I became convinced that many of the difficult questions posed by the history of Brazil during the period in question could be at least partially answered if one studied more carefully the full implications of this import substitution process. On further contemplation, it seemed to me that the same was true with regard to the other countries of Latin America, and to the "underdeveloped" world in general.

The argument of this book, therefore, suggests that the generalizations offered here are of general applicability to the developing nations. However, I recognize that two factors may confuse the issue of whether the thesis is valid outside of Latin America. For one thing, as a group the Latin

American countries are more advanced along the road to development and economic diversification than are most of the other underdeveloped areas, and it is possible to argue that countries considerably behind Latin America will not inevitably follow the path which it has trod.

In the second place, in a number of countries of Africa and Asia development has gone forward during the last two decades under the aegis of a supposed "socialist" development strategy. In some instances (of course, I am referring to nations outside of the bloc controlled by Communist parties), state participation in development has certainly been greater than is generally the case in Latin America. However, the supposed "socialist" ideology is frequently not much more than window dressing, and the import substitution type of development rather than what I've called in this volume the "Soviet" strategy has in fact been used.

Naturally, I owe many debts of gratitude for help in developing the ideas contained in this book and for aid in converting it from an idea to a printed volume. Discussions with several Brazilian economists, particularly Ignacio Rangel and Mario Simonsen, were very important in bringing to my attention the fundamental importance of import substitution and many of the implications of the process. Further help in refining some of these ideas was received in discussions with American economists Werner Baer and James Street. Criticisms offered by some of my Rutgers colleagues, particularly Monroe Berkowitz and Richard Blackhurst, helped me to sharpen many of my arguments.

Thanks are also due to Mrs. John Carman for typing the manuscript, as well as to Orbis Books for seeing the volume through the editorial process. Finally, the patience of my wife, Joan, and my children, Meg and Tony, is much appreciated. They were tolerant of too much discussion of the subject of the book and too much of my bending over the typewriter when certainly they would have preferred that I be talking to or playing with them.

A NEW DEVELOPMENT STRATEGY

Introduction

Economists tend to follow certain fads or fashions in the subject matter of their research and writings. Usually, these are closely connected with the problems which appear to be most urgent at a particular moment. During the 1930s, and up to about 1950, attention tended to be centered on the issues involved in maintaining a stable economy and avoiding the alternatives of boom and bust. By the 1950s, when the business cycle problem finally appeared to be largely resolved, due at least in part to the ideas which the economists had elaborated, concentration shifted largely to the issues of economic development. By the following decade, the economists' attention had shifted once again (at least in the United States) to a fascination with the issues of economic inequality, income maintenance, and discrimination; and with the technical possibilities of theorizing and testing hypotheses raised by the advent of the electronic computer. Even more recently, the economies of pollution, conservation, inflation, and recession have come into vogue.

Although discussion of economic development has now moved somewhat off the center of the stage, we feel there are several reasons why economists should pay a considerable part of their attention to the issues associated with it. First, the problem is still with us, with two-thirds of the world's population continuing to live in countries which are "underdeveloped." Second, much of what has been written in the

3

field is not very satisfactory, and seems to reflect much greater knowledge of classical and neoclassical economic theory than of the actual problems of the underdeveloped nations. Finally, it is our conviction that a good deal of value still remains to be said on the subject.

Why Industrialize?

In this book we shall take for granted the desirability of development and of at least some degree of industrialization in each of the present underdeveloped nations. We shall have something to say about the factors which will limit the possibilities of industrialization for any given country. We shall also discuss the limitations of what we shall call the "Castro" strategy of development, which puts primary emphasis for a considerable period of time on the expansion of export agriculture in the developing countries. Finally, we shall note at various points the interrelationships between the development of manufacturing and that of agriculture.

Fundamentally, we shall accept the advisability of some degree of industrialization. Nevertheless, it may be of some use at this point to deal with the anti-industrialization prejudices which still persist among economists and politicians in the highly developed countries, when they are dealing with the underdeveloped nations.

Herman Finer has stated the anti-industrialization case as well as anyone, in his contribution to Williamson and Buttrick's well-known volume *Economic Development: Principles and Patterns*. There, in discussing tariffs, he wrote:

> Policies promoting national self-sufficiency have been instituted. . . . Latin America, underdeveloped, has stimulated native industries of iron and steel, cement and metal processing, for this same reason, instead of buying from the most efficient producers. They lose as consumers more than they gain for defense purposes or in national pride, for they can

hardly prevail against big nations—yet their envy and pride are directed more toward their own more comparable neighbors. Further, they are proud that they can manufacture as well as the renowned industrial nations. This causes underdeveloped countries everywhere to entertain grandiose ideas of industrialization, and to be tempted to undertake works far too expensive for the stage at which they now are.

Home industries and agriculture are protected and are required to employ nationals against competition from advance and development elsewhere. This is another species of monopoly and has its usual effects; intense nationalism fosters protection which private interests exploit for their own advantage. An artificial economic structure is built. It is not because the government exists that tariffs come into being, but because economic groups use government as a cat's-paw. They have riddled the political process with specious pleas of national advantage and perverted reason.

Where other national economies produce at less cost, the home entrepreneur asks government for tariffs in order to equalize the costs of production. The consumer is mulcted of the advantage of lower costs. The producer in the protected country loses markets in the lower-cost rival's territory. The least efficient producers are subsidized at the cost of economic development.[1]

The fundamental presupposition of Professor Finer's analysis is that the consumers of the underdeveloped country would in fact be able to purchase the manufactured goods they need from the highly industrialized countries. There is no recognition of the fact, which is fundamental to the relations between the developed and underdeveloped nations in the present world, that the ability of the underdeveloped countries to buy the products of the industrial ones depends fundamentally on the willingness of the highly developed countries to buy the raw materials and foodstuffs of the underdeveloped nations, and that there is no similar reciprocal relationship. Thus, to give an example: Chile's ability to purchase manufactured goods from the United States depends on the willingness of the United States to purchase her copper; but the ability of the United States to purchase copper depends virtually not at all on the willingness of Chile to buy manufactured goods made in the United States.

Hence, the consumers of the underdeveloped country may not in fact be faced with the choice of buying cheaper goods from the United States or more expensive goods made at home; but rather one of either purchasing goods made at home, or not being able to purchase at all the quantity of goods they would like to buy and possess the national currency to purchase. In such a case, if consumer demand is to be met adequately, it will have to be met by national production, or not at all.

In his pioneer statement in 1950 as Secretary General of the Economic Commission for Latin America, *The Economic Development of Latin America and Its Principal Problems,* Raul Prebisch summed up the role of industrialization in the presently underdeveloped countries. What he says of Latin America is equally applicable to the rest of the underdeveloped world. He comments:

> Hence, the fundamental significance of the industrialization of the new countries. Industrialization is not an end in itself, but the principal means at the disposal of those countries of obtaining a share of the benefits of technical progress and of progressively raising the standard of living of the masses. (p. 2)

> Formerly, before the great depression, development in the Latin American countries was stimulated from abroad by the constant increase of exports. There is no reason to suppose, at least at present, that this will again occur to the same extent, except under very exceptional circumstances. These countries no longer have an alternative between vigorous growth along those lines and internal expansion through industrialization. Industrialization has become the most important means of expansion.[2]

In addition, there is another implied presumption in Professor Finer's comments. This is that there is full employment in the underdeveloped country, and that that nation is faced with the diversion of labor and other resources already employed in the most productive way possible to some less productive use in order to industrialize.

However, this is far from the fact in today's underdeveloped nations. These nations are faced with extensive underemployment of their people and of their natural resources. A sizable part of their population is engaged in doing work which makes little or no net contribution to the gross national product. In addition, these countries generally have rapidly growing populations.

In theory, of course, these underemployed workers and the new ones coming into the labor market in ever increasing quantities could be employed in agriculture. However, as we shall note elsewhere in this book, the possibility of expanding the production of the segment of their agriculture devoted to exports is severely limited by the inelastic markets for these products in the highly industrialized nations. The expansion of that part of agriculture devoted to serving the national market is also limited by several factors. First, it requires the introduction of large quantities of agricultural implements and machinery, as well as fertilizers, insecticides, and technical know-how, virtually all of which must be imported from abroad. But without the ability to increase exports or decrease imports, such investments will be very hard, if not impossible, to undertake. Second, such improvement of domestically oriented agriculture usually will require a redistribution of land ownership; but the political power of traditional large landowners will be too great to make this possible until the urban areas have grown in economic prosperity and political influence, something which is not likely to occur very rapidly without considerable industrialization. Third, the cultural traditions of the rural areas will usually be such that there will be great resistance from even small landholders to using modern methods until the urban economy has grown sufficiently to exercise a "demonstration effect" on the rural folk and convince them of the need for such changes. The best way to bring this about is for the urban sector of the national economy to be able to produce the consumer goods which will provide the best incentive for subsistence farmers to turn to production for the market. For such consumer goods to come from abroad, it would be necessary to strain beyond the breaking point already overburdened foreign exchange budgets.

Finally, there is the problem of the rapid growth of the cities in the underdeveloped countries, which is tending to outstrip the ability of these urban centers to provide migrants from the interior with jobs or with adequate public services. If these nations don't produce a sizable quantity of the goods and services needed by these new city residents, these goods and services will represent a massive addition to the demands on these countries' limited quantities of foreign exchange—without adding to their ability to acquire more foreign exchange.

Hence, there is ample justification for industrialization. In any case, discussion of the issue is virtually irrelevant, insofar as we are concerned. Public opinion in the underdeveloped countries is generally convinced of the need for industrialization, and the governments of all these nations are committed to encouraging it.

Before leaving this issue, however, it might be well to note one other aspect of Finer's indictment of industrialization: his accusation that much of the industrialization effort is devoted to enterprises which are "far too expensive for the state at which they now are." There may be some projects against which this charge is valid. However, Albert Hirschman has pointed out that many of the industrial projects which appear to be overly ambitious, and to involve excessive capital investment, have great value in accumulating skills useful in various parts of the economy, as well as in instilling the "maintenance habit" in people who are unaccustomed to the need for taking close care of capital goods, whose constant upkeep is not immediately apparent.

In addition, some of the kinds of industries condemned by Finer may be justified by noneconomic considerations, such as the need for fomenting a "developmentalist" psychology among the populace. However, the prevalence of such projects is not as great as Finer implies. Furthermore, as we shall indicate in our discussion of import substitution as a strategy of development, industrialization frequently tends to have a more or less natural chain of evolution, moving from simpler enterprises producing light consumer goods, to more complex ones turning out heavier products.

Economists and Import Substitution

Most of those who have written about economic development have tended to concentrate their attention on problems concerned with the supply of goods and services in the developing nations' economies. Thus, they have dealt with the problem of capital accumulation and related issues such as the availability of savings, foreign investment, interest rates, and the underdeveloped nations' ability to obtain financial resources from international lending agencies; with the development of an adequate labor force, through education, on-the-job training, and other measures; and with the stimulation of entrepreneurship and the provision of an adequate managerial force.

The author has dealt with many of these issues in an earlier book.[3] However, in the present volume we are concerned rather with the demand side of the development equation. Our attention is concentrated upon a particular strategy of economic development is the paucity of savings, as is argued mand for the goods produced as a result of the industrialization process. We will analyze the effect of the existence of this assured demand on the general development process. We will try to explore the limits of this import substitution market and show how other sources of demand can be found once the possibility of generating demand through import substitution has been exhausted.

We think that this approach to the subject is of basic importance, because we do not believe that the key issue of economic development is the paucity of savings, as is argued by many writers on the subject. We agree with Albert Hirschman that in most underdeveloped countries there is a sizable amount of savings available, which tends to go into unproductive channels such as purchase of rural land, urban real estate, or bank accounts abroad. We also agree that with proper incentive there will be much more savings generated than is apparent before the process of development begins. The basic problem with regard to savings and investment in the developing countries is the stimulation of incentive and the generation of a sufficient number of attractive opportunities for investment in fields which contribute to development. Import substitution helps to provide such incentive and opportunities.

Thus entrepreneurship, the mobilization and organization of savings and other elements of production, is of key importance to economic development. The development of entrepreneurship is hampered by a number of things: cultural factors which militate against it, lack of know-how, lack of experience, lack of markets. The import substitution strategy, as we shall indicate, provides a market, allows entrepreneurs the opportunity to get experience and know-how, and gives time for the cultural factors to be modified in the direction of emphasizing the virtues of entrepreneurship.

Surprisingly little attention has been paid to the import substitution phenomenon by those economists of the developed countries concerned with the problems of economic development. Some of them, such as Ragnar Nurkse, W. Arthur Lewis, Gunnar Myrdal, Hans Singer, and Everett Hagen, have given qualified support to the ideas, and Albert Hirschman has been a good deal more emphatic in his approval. Others, such as Gerald Meier and Harry Johnson have taken a more or less hostile attitude toward the phenomenon.

The ECLA Import Substitution Argument

The dynamic group of economists associated with the Economic Commission for Latin America (ECLA) of the United Nations has taken the lead in developing the idea of an import substitution strategy of development. Through their studies of the development of the economies of this area, particularly since the Great Depression of the 1930s, they have worked out a description of the import substitution process and have analyzed some of its characteristics. Although what they write about the phenomenon is based on what has occurred in only one segment of the "third world," much of what they say, as we shall see, is also applicable to other developing countries.

One of the clearest and most succinct summations of the ECLA thesis on import substitution is to be found in Maria Concepção Tavares' article, "Rise and Decline of Import Substitution in Brazil," which appeared in the March 1964 issue of ECLA's *Economic Bulletin of Latin America*. We may regard it as a typical review of the issue in terms of ECLA's analysis.

Tavares begins her study with a review of the development of the export sector of the Latin American economies, which gave rise to a kind of "dual economy," a contrast between the dynamic monetary sector associated with exports and the virtually stagnant subsistence economy in which, in most cases, the great majority of the population continued to be located.

The writer notes that it was interferences with the export economy, particularly the Great Depression of the 1930s (but also two world wars), which set in motion the process of import substitution. Faced with a sudden fall in the quantity and value of their exports, the governments of the Latin American countries sought to protect their nations against the internal impact of these events. They did so by rationing foreign exchange, devaluing their currencies, and buying up the unsalable surpluses of their major export products. These measures served to provide a kind of natural protection for new industries designed to provide the goods which could no longer be imported, while at the same time maintaining internal purchasing power in these countries.

The first period of import substitution, according to Tavares, continued through 1945, with World War Two resulting in even more restrictions on the ability of the Latin American countries to import than had the Great Depression. However, between 1945 and 1954 these nations once more found that they had a relatively favorable export position. The demand for their products was high, and prices recovered considerably from the low points they had reached during the Great Depression. For this decade, therefore, Tavares argues, most of the countries tended to turn once more toward an externally oriented economy, although a few of them took advantage of their high export income to import large quantitites of capital goods and thus to forward the process of industrialization.

After 1954, the prices of Latin American primary exports again fell, and the process of import substitution was, of necessity, intensified. The situation continued to exist at the time Tavares wrote her article.

Hence, the ECLA argument as to the cause of the adoption of the import substitution strategy is that it was forced upon the Latin American countries by the catastrophic decline in their export income and ability to import during the Great Depression and World War Two. However, Tavares observes that most of the countries developed during this period more or less deliberate policies of import substitution.

Tavares notes that there are various meanings which

might be given to the idea of "import substitution," and even suggests that it is not a very happy phrase, but that she uses it because it has won general currency as a result of the publications of ECLA and others. She underlines the idea that the phrase does not mean "to eliminate *all* imports, that is, arrive at autarchy." Quite to the contrary, as a result of the substitution of certain imports there will arise a demand for others—the raw materials and intermediary goods entering into the production of import substitutes.

The writer notes the difference between "apparent" and "real" import substitution, and different possible relationships between these. In one case, it is possible to conceive of a situation in which the actual composition of imports does not change, but in which national producers share with importers the sales of an increasing market for various manufactured goods. In this instance, she comments, there would be no apparent import substitution, although the importance of imports in the general economy would decline.

A second alternative would be one in which new products, which had not hitherto been imported, began to be produced in a given country. In such a case there would be no substitution for previous imports, but rather a prevention of imports and "a new modification of the pattern of division of social labor of the economy."

Another very frequent case, she says, might be the decline of importation of "non-essential" goods, "to adjust the general level of imports to the effective capacity to import," as a result of which there would "begin to be a stimulus to the internal production of those goods." In this instance, she notes that the "real" substitution would be produced after the "apparent" decline in imports.

Finally, the writer mentions the frequent cases in which the "real" decline in imports is much less than the "apparent" decline. This occurs when the introduction of a new industry to replace imports gives rise to a large demand for the raw materials and other products used by this industry.

Tavares states that "in the first phases of the process of substitution, the selection of new lines of production is made in the light of existing internal demand for those elements which are easiest to substitute, which are . . . finished consumers' goods." Thereafter, however, she argues, "it may be that there is an attempt to substitute simultaneously in various categories, although with different intensity in certain groups of products in accordance with the specific conditions of each country and with the stage of development in which it is."

This planning of the different stages of import substitution must not be determined, Tavares says, by a merely "static" vision of the economy, but rather must take into account the likely expansion of the market arising from the process of import substitution itself. Furthermore, it will depend considerably on the state of the nation's export markets; a situation of absolute stagnation of exports will make import substitution industrialization very difficult, because it may well be necessary actually to increase imports at certain periods in the process.

There are certain internal conditioning factors which will influence the process of import substitution. Tavares lists these as "the size and structure of the national markets, the nature of technological evolution, and the constellation of productive resources." In connection with the first of these, the writer notes that the process of import substitution itself will increase the market "in two ways, as much by the increase in income of the high income groups as by the incorporation in consumption of industrial and allied goods and services of the wage workers brought into the new dynamic sectors. . . . " However, she states that when the process comes to involve the production of durable consumer goods, the market will have to depend largely on the high income groups in the economy.

Technological factors will tend to reduce the impact of import substitution industrialization on employment, according to Tavares. There will be a tendency to adopt the latest modern technology, which uses a relatively small labor force, a fact which in itself may limit the market to more complicated kinds of import substitutes. This is a tendency which for various reasons she does not think can be overcome.

Finally, with regard to the available productive resources, Tavares says that in the process of industrialization there is a tendency to use large quantities of relatively scarce resources, such as capital and skilled labor, and relatively small quantities of the more abundant kind. This situation is made worse by the relative lack of change in the rural sector of the economy. In addition, every one of the Latin American countries is faced with a shortage of one or another of the natural resources required for industrialization.

The last part of Tavares' analysis of the import substitution model of development deals with certain criticisms which have been made of this model. First, she notes the allegation that import substitution tends to encourage a high degree of monopoly in the industrial sector, which in turn adds to the costs and prices of products produced by that sector. She argues that a mere comparison of costs of production in the developing country with those in an already industrialized nation is not adequate; that a comparison should be made which involves "a macroeconomic relationship which takes into account social gains and costs." Furthermore, she suggests that it is doubtful that most of the high costs of production in the developing countries come from monopoly; on the contrary, given the size of the available markets, monopoly may frequently be the best way to lower costs, through providing the economies of large-scale production.

Tavares again deals with the problem that manufacturing enterprises do not absorb enough of the labor supply. She suggests that within the framework of the import substitution model the only way to deal with this is the absorption of labor into services and into government employment in public works, and notes that both of these methods of handling the problem are widespread in Latin America.

Finally, she cites the problem of a lack of programming in Latin American development and notes that such planning on the part of governments increases as substitution advances. In summarizing this point, she says that "it is not sufficient to wait for the dynamics of this type of development to bring about by itself a modification of macroeconomic functions of production which would permit national integration, with absorption of surplus labor and improvement of the distribution of income from the personal, sectorial and regional point of view."

Foreseeing what we in this book have referred to as the "post-import or substitution crisis," Tavares comments:

> It appears, then, that if those objectives are not deliberately pursued, the process will lead to an even greater aggravation of the basic structural duality of the Latin American economies, that is, a widening of the existing breach between the "capitalist sector," relatively developed, and the "subsistence sector," extremely underdeveloped. This would not only prevent that the former act as a dynamic motor of the system in general, but very probably would end by putting a brake on its own internal dynamism.

In recent years, some of those who were originally most enthusiastic about import substitution have tended to cast doubts on its efficacy. Even Raul Prebisch, in his book *Transformación y desarrollo: La gran tarea de la América Latina,* expresses disappointment that import substitution industrialization has not provided more jobs, has sometimes involved excessive degrees of protectionism, and has not provided adequately large markets in many cases. He has commented: "In our opinion, that development cannot be based solely on import substitution, but also on a great effort to export to the rest of the world, and especially on a regional basis."[4]

As later parts of the present book will indicate, we have no quarrel with these observations of Prebisch. However, we would suggest that his disappointment with import substitution might have been less had he realized that import substitution is part of a continuing process of development, one phase which by itself will seldom, if ever, produce a highly developed, general industrialized economy.

Conclusion

Even the ECLA economists have not fully investigated all the implications of the import substitution strategy. They have not explored the wide range of effects which the existence of a market assured by the import substitution process has on the economy in general, as well as on the society and the political structure of a developing country which is using this strategy. They have not thoroughly looked into its prerequisites and what comes after it. These are a few of the issues which we will deal with in the pages which follow.

NOTES

1. Harold F. Williamson and John A. Buttrick, eds., *Economic Development: Principles and Patterns* (New York: Prentice-Hall, 1954), p. 399.

2. Raul Prebisch, *The Economic Development of Latin America and Its Principal Problems* (Lake Success, N.Y.: United Nations, 1950), pp. 2 and 4.

3. Robert J. Alexander, *A Primer of Economic Development* (New York: Macmillan, 1962).

4. Raul Prebisch, *Transformación y desarrollo: La gran tarea de la América Latina* (Mexico: Fondo de Cultura Económica, 1970), p. 52.

CHAPTER ONE

Alternative Development Strategies

Each nation's path to development and "modernization" is to a certain degree unique. The individual characteristics of each country will determine what strategy of economic development its leaders will adopt. However, an underdeveloped country which is seeking economic development and industrialization in the final quarter of the twentieth century has a number of basic alternative strategies to choose from among those which have been used historically and those which are being employed by contemporary nations.

British Strategy of Development

The first modern industrial nation was Great Britain. She followed her own strategy of industrialization which her unique position as the world's first modern manufacturing country made possible. Her example of development is of relatively little value to contemporary countries which are seeking a model for industrialization.

The basic characteristic of the British strategy of economic development, which might also be called the "manufacture export strategy,"[1] was that it was based largely on the exportation of the manufactured products which were turned out by her pioneer industries. It was these exports which largely provided the "motor force" and resources for the expansion of the development process.

There were several factors which made it possible for Great Britain to use the strategy of development which it adopted. The nature of these factors indicates why such a strategy is of use to only a comparatively small number of developing countries in the world of the twentieth century.

The first and most basic factor about the British strategy of development is that Great Britain was the first modern industrial nation. The first Industrial Revolution took place in that country, starting around the middle of the eighteenth century, and for almost a century Great Britain had little or no competition as the producer and exporter of manufactured products. Her steam-driven mechanized factories turned out textiles, metallurgical products, and other industrial goods at cheap prices which were hard for less advanced producers in other countries to meet. Hence Britain was able to flood her former American colonies, her Indian empire, the former Spanish and Portuguese colonies as they gained independence early in the nineteenth century, and much of continental Europe, with the output of her rapidly multiplying factories.

The spread of British commerce in manufactured goods was matched by the growth in popularity of economic ideas which largely originated in Great Britain, and the latter facilitated the former. These were the concepts of laissez-faire and free trade, developed by Adam Smith, David Ricardo, and their successors, which stressed that it was "unnatural" and "unscientific" for a country to raise barriers to the entry into its borders of manufactured goods produced in another nation which had a "comparative advantage" in manufacturing these commodities.

The British development strategy had a logical sequence of its own. The first products of British manufacturers which found ready markets abroad were textiles, hats, and clothing. They swamped the markets of India, destroying much of the traditional hand-spinning and weaving industries, and causing real distress in thousands of villages of the subcontinent. They also provided cheap clothing for the slave plantations of the Southern United States, the West Indies, and Brazil, as well as goods to exchange for slaves, ivory, and other valuable products from Africa. In this same period light metallurgical products from Britain such as household utensils, tips for ploughs, and other goods also found a ready market in many parts of the world.

However, in time, as railroads spread throughout the globe about the middle of the nineteenth century, and as some other countries began to industrialize, heavier metallurgical products became major staples of the British export trade. British rails and rolling stock, British textile machinery and mining equipment, British steamships and telegraph equipment joined textiles and clothing among the goods sold throughout the world.

Another characteristic of the British strategy of development was that it involved a long period of what might be called "incubation" of industrialization. The predecessor of factory industry, the "putting-out system," in which merchants supplied raw materials to the farmers and villagers who worked these materials in their own homes, grew for more than two centuries before factories developed. Even then, these "manufactories," as Adam Smith called them, were merely the gathering together of handicraftsmen under one roof and under the direction of a single entrepreneur. It took two generations at least before these were converted into establishments in which machines were harnessed to water power and then to steam, and the Industrial Revolution was fully underway.

This long period of development in a world in which there did not exist any other industrialized nation meant that British industrialization could proceed through its own process of trial and error, with relatively little influence from outside. The capital equipment and technical knowledge needed for the putting-out system and then for manufacturing could be developed as they were needed. There was no "revolution of rising expectations." There was no "demonstration effect" of much higher levels of living existing in already industrialized countries putting pressure on Britain to hasten the process of its own industrialization, since no other models of an industrialized country existed.

The British strategy of economic development is not one which can be widely copied in the final quarter of the twentieth century. No present-day developing country can be the first industrialized nation, for many others already exist. In virtually all cases, the new manufacturing enterprises of the developing countries can produce only at costs much superior to those of their counterparts in the already industrialized countries. Furthermore, the manufactured goods of the developing countries generally face greater (or lesser) government-imposed barriers to entry into the already developed nations.

In addition, the presently underdeveloped countries do not live in the same time dimension as Britain did in the fifteenth through eighteenth centuries. They live in a world in which the material advantages which the industrialized countries have gained for being industrialized become widely known even in the underdeveloped ones. They cannot follow the prescription of the ideological descendants of Adam Smith and wait until the forces of world trade have so changed as to give them a "comparative advantage" in manufacturing, thus providing them with the "natural" ability to compete with the already industrialized countries in the world market in the production of manufactured goods, a process which in some cases might take as many centuries as did Britain's own industrialization, and in other instances might not occur at all.

Thus developing countries today have to depend largely on their own populations for markets for the output of their new manufacturing enterprises, at least in the beginning. Only in the rare case in which underdeveloped nations have special relations with already industrialized countries, which not only give the former immediate access to the markets of the latter, but also give them the possibility of making full use of the technical and managerial ability of the industrialized nations, can a country use the British strategy of economic development. There are a few such cases in the contemporary world—Puerto Rico, to a limited degree Surinam, and to an even more circumscribed extent some of the former French colonies in Africa about exhaust the list of such nations.

Soviet or "Forced Capitalization" Strategy of Development

Another strategy of development more relevant to the world of the final quarter of the twentieth century is that used by the Soviet Union. Within a generation, the methods used by Stalin and his successors converted the Union of Soviet Socialist Republics from the least industrialized of the large European powers into the second largest industrial power on the globe. Subsequent to World War Two, this same strategy was also used to a greater or lesser degree by eight East European countries, China, Outer Mongolia, North Korea, and North Vietnam.

Several elements are essential parts of the Soviet strategy of development. These include state ownership of most of the economy and state control of virtually all of it, minute and detailed planning, a very high degree of concentration on the accumulation of heavy capital goods, and the use of extensive force to keep down the demands of the populace for consumer goods.

The Soviet strategy of development provides for the state to own all industrial enterprises, as well as mines, transport and communication facilities, and foreign commerce. Although most of agriculture and part of retail trade is considered by the Soviet ideologues to be cooperative rather than state enterprise, this is looked upon as a transitory state, tolerated for political rather than ideological reasons, and in any case effective state control over so-called collective farmers is only a little less complete than control over the government-owned state farms.

This strategy of development also provides for very extensive planning, presumably to the end of making the most efficient possible use of the economy's resources for the purpose of development. This involves the most detailed calculations of the expected factor needs and output of virtually every factory and farm in the economy, as well as similar computations for every commercial enterprise and service facility. It also provides for coordination of all these individual planning projects into a nationwide economic plan covering a varying number of years. Incentives within the economy are directed toward fulfillment of the plan.

The third element in the Soviet strategy of development is its concentration on the accumulation of heavy capital goods. Not only in the Soviet Union, but also in most of the other states using this strategy, the overwhelming emphasis of each successive plan has been on the building of steel plants, giant electric projects, mining enterprises, long-range transport facilities, heavy machinery enterprises, and similar projects. The establishment of a consumer goods industry and the development of agriculture—except for that part that produces industrial raw materials—has consistently received low priority. In addition, there has regularly been much greater insistence on fulfillment of the plan in the fields of heavy capital goods than in those parts of the economy serving the consumer.

Finally, an essential element of the Soviet strategy of development is the political regime which makes it possible to prevent the growth of any effective dissent from the fulfillment of the plan, and particularly to check the development of any effective political and economic demand for more consumer commodities rather than for more heavy production goods. This regime includes a single political party which is conceived to have a metaphysical right to govern because it supposedly represents the class which is destined by history to be the ultimate ruler of society. It includes the complete suppression of all vehicles of expression which might diverge from the official policy; it includes the imposition of extreme forms of discipline on the work force, including limitations on income, public obloquy, and even concentration camps and the threat of death, with little opportunity being presented to the workers to defend their own rights.

The costs of the Soviet strategy of development are very high. They include a longer or shorter period during which the consumers receive little or no benefit from the country's industrialization. They include a degree of political tyranny, suppression of individual rights, dictatorship by a self-chosen few which has been equalled in modern times, perhaps, only by the Nazi dictatorship of Adolf Hitler. Although those advocating this strategy of development seldom recount its costs, they are widely known in the underdeveloped countries, and few countries except those which have come under the control of a Communist party have desired to pay these costs.

Castro, or "Primary Product Effort," Strategy of Economic Development

The third road to economic development which exists in the world of the 1970s is that which the Cuban regime of Fidel Castro followed after 1964. It involves a nation concentrating its efforts in the first phase on the development of its traditional basic agricultural or mineral export in order to acquire the resources which will permit it to bring in from abroad those capital and managerial resources necessary for the industrialization process.

The Castro government adopted this policy only after short flirtations with the import substitution and Soviet strategies of development. However, there is at least some evidence that in the mid-1960s the Soviet Union began to recommend it to a number of countries outside the Communist bloc, and that the U.S.S.R.'s pressure was largely responsible for its adoption in Cuba itself.

Interestingly enough, what we are calling the Castro strategy of economic development finds favor among numerous economists in the non-Communist industrial countries. Following the path first trod by Adam Smith, they argue that underdeveloped countries which desire to stimulate rapid growth of their economies should concentrate on those aspects of the economy in which they have a "comparative advantage."[2]

However, there are strong reasons for believing that although this advice was valuable for nations seeking rapid development in the nineteenth century, it is of considerably less validity for developing countries in the final quarter of the twentieth century. The late Ragnar Nurkse has pointed out at some length the changes during the last hundred years which have made this strategy of development less efficacious at present than it was a century before.

As Nurkse notes, trade was an "engine of development" during the nineteenth century because of the increased demand of the industrialized countries for raw materials and foodstuffs from the underdeveloped ones, which brought the beginning of development to the latter group of countries, attracting foreign investment at the same time that it brought a demand for exports. This affected principally the temperate area zones with immigrant peoples from Europe.

After 1914, however, there was a decline in the growth of demand for raw material and food exports from the underdeveloped countries to the industrialized ones. The demand for raw materials and foodstuffs did not keep up with the increase in international trade, with world production, and with industrial production.

Nurkse has observed that this change came about for a variety of reasons. First, production in the highly developed nations shifted from light to heavy industries, particularly the engineering and chemical industries, and thus from industries with high raw material content to those with a low percentage of raw materials. A second factor was the rising share in the output of the highly industrialized nations of services, which call for no contributions from the exporters of basic agricultural and mineral products.

A third factor which reduced the potency of export of basic commodities as an "engine of development" was the low-income elasticity of consumer demand for agricultural products in the developed countries. With their high level of income, those countries tend to spend only a small proportion of any increase in their incomes on food, and hence on agricultural products.

A fourth factor militating against the expansion of traditional exports serving as a motor force for development was the fact that most highly industrialized nations have established more or less high protection for their agriculture, and in some cases for their mining. Not only the United States but the nations of the European Economic Community and various manufacturing nations have subsidized their agriculture and exports of its products.

A fifth important reason for the decline of traditional exports as the principal vehicle for development, according to Nurkse, was the fact that substantial economies have been achieved in the highly industrialized countries in the use of natural materials in industrial processes. Not only are smaller overall quantities of raw materials required now than was true a few decades ago, but in addition the highly industrialized countries have to an increasing degree used synthetics and substitutes produced at home instead of the agricultural and mineral raw materials imported from the underdeveloped nations.

As a result of all of these factors, Nurkse noted that the possibility of development through the expansion of basic agricultural and mineral exports was not very good, because the demand for these products increased less rapidly than the ability of the underdeveloped countries to produce them. The upshot was likely to be that concentration in this field would result in an underdeveloped country producing a larger amount of its export produce for less income than it would have received for a smaller amount.[3]

The "oil crisis" of 1973–1974 and the rise in prices of a number of other key raw materials and foodstuffs may possibly represent a reversal of some of the trends noted by Nurkse. However, it is as yet too early to know whether the increase in demand for these products relative to supply is permanent; it may well be that the highly industrialized countries will find ways through technological development to circumvent the high prices of many raw materials and foodstuffs.

However, there are additional reasons, not discussed by Nurkse, which weigh in the balance against the use of the export of traditional foodstuffs and raw materials as the "engine of development" in the late twentieth century. One of these is the high degree of instability which very heavy dependence upon the export of agricultural products and minerals is likely to produce in the economy of an underdeveloped country. The prices of these products vary frequently and extremely, and the underdeveloped countries are likely to have limited ability to control these variations of price. Hence, the general economy of the underdeveloped country is likely to be subject to frequent alternations of boom and bust, government finances will be highly unpredictable, and in general the possibilities of rational economic calculation in the economy will be severely limited.

Albert Hirschman has suggested another disadvantage of what we have called the "Castro" strategy of development. This is the fact that it does not provide the backward and forward linkages which in the process of import substitution give great impetus to the continuation of the industrialization process. The intensification of the export of a raw material or foodstuff does not give rise to the demand for component parts which might give rise to the establishment of enterprises to produce such components; nor does it generate within the developing country new manufacturing or even commercial activity in connection with distributing these raw material or foodstuff exports.

There is also the fact that heavy dependence on the export of a limited number of agricultural and mineral products is likely to limit the "economic independence" of the underdeveloped country. In most such cases, the nation involved does the great bulk of its exporting to one or two major buyers of its products. The industrial purchaser of its goods will in most instances have readily available alternate sources of supply, but it will be very difficult for the raw material and foodstuff exporter to find alternate purchasers for its goods. Hence, the major economic interests and the government of the underdeveloped country are likely to be subject to extensive pressure from both the immediate purchasers of its goods and the government of the country in which these purchasers are located. In an age of strong nationalism such as is the second half of the twentieth century, such a situation is not likely to be relished by public opinion or the government of any underdeveloped nation.

Of course, all this does not mean that economic development is to be found through a destruction of the traditional export sectors of the economy of the developing country. As we shall see elsewhere in this volume, the development of a sizable export trade and its complement, appreciable quantities of imports, is an essential prerequisite for the use of the import substitution strategy of development. In addition, there may be exceptional cases in which a nation may be able to use the Castro strategy of development. This might be true if its export of a given agricultural and mineral product constituted a comparatively small part of the world total. In such a case it may be able to make what for it is a major increase in output and export of its products without influencing significantly the world price of that commodity. Use of this strategy might also be practicable if a purchaser was willing for noneconomic reasons to take all of an underdeveloped country's export product.

However, in general, a strategy of economic development which would rely principally upon a large expansion of traditional exports as the "engine of development" is of limited use in the late twentieth-century world. It is not a very reliable basis for the relatively rapid development of a rounded modern economy.

NOTES

1. I owe to my graduate student Joel Sokoloff the suggestions for alternate development strategies which I have labeled "British," "Soviet," and "Castro."

2. It is ironic to note the coincidence of economic policy carried out by the most left-wing of the world Communist leaders and that advocated by the most conservative "capitalist" economists.

3. See Ragnar Nurkse's *Problems of Capital Formation in Underdeveloped Countries and Patterns of Trade and Development* (New York: Oxford University Press, 1967).

CHAPTER TWO

The Import Substitution Strategy

The fourth strategy of development is that based on industrialization through the establishment of enterprises producing goods which were formerly imported. This is the strategy which is being used knowingly or unwittingly by the majority of the developing countries at the present time.

There are two prerequisites to this strategy of development. First, a country must have a substantial amount of imports, which means that it must have passed through the phase of development in which it has constructed an important agricultural or mineral export sector. It is only through the export-oriented segment of the economy that there can be generated the foreign exchange required to purchase imports.

The second prerequisite for the use of the import substitution strategy is protection for the new manufacturing industries which are to produce the goods that take the place of commodities formerly brought in from abroad. Since in all likelihood the costs of these new manufacturing enterprises will be higher than those of similar firms in the already established industrial countries, the new factories will have to be protected from outside competition if they are to come into existence at all.

Captive Market

If these two prerequisites are met, the developing country is faced with a situation in which there exists a captive market for those firms within its borders which are producing certain manufactured goods. Furthermore, the size of that market is known since it has hitherto been taken care of by imports, the statistics of which are likely to be relatively good, since the governments of most underdeveloped countries, which depend on agricultural or mineral exports, rely very heavily on taxation of both exports and imports for their revenue.

Many who have written about economic development have not seen this importance of existing markets during the import substitution phase of industrialization. Thus Stephen Enke, who regards government-protected industrialization as "forced," in his well-known study *The Economics for Development* has asked:

> Who will be willing and able to buy the output resulting from forced industrial expansion? Industrial workers cannot buy it all. Their total pay will be less than total costs of industrial production. And some, if not most of their wages must buy foods. There is a limit to the total demand of an agricultural sector for the output of domestic industry. Of course there is always an export demand—but often only at a price below domestic unit costs of production—so this is not a sure solution.[1]

This passage, of course, overlooks the fact that when the so-called forced industrial growth is for the purpose of meeting a need previously met by imports, there *does* exist a market. Indeed, as a result of the existence of such an import-created market, the process of development is not faced during the import substitution period with the question of who is going to buy the newly produced manufactured goods. Those who formerly bought imported goods are going to do so. Rather, the major problem is what might be called the "physical" one of how to build the productive capacity and to provide the manpower needs to meet the demand of a market the size of which is already known.

Furthermore, the very process of import substitution development tends to expand for some time more or less automatically the existing market. The employment of labor in the new factories brings new elements into the market economy. Most of the new industrial workers are people who had been earning little or no money income before being employed in manufacturing.

In addition, the import substitution process tends for an extended period to expand the possibilities of import substitution itself. The establishment of one branch of industry will generate demand for processed raw materials, intermediate goods, machinery, and other requirements which in the first instance will be met by imports. When and if the size of this demand becomes sufficiently large to justify the establishment of a firm within the country to produce these semiprocessed and capital goods, an additional possibility for import substitution will have been created.

The import substitution strategy also provides a certain degree of self-perpetuation because of backward and forward linkages, as Albert Hirschman has shown. Perhaps the automobile industry is the most dramatic example of this. When auto assembly plants are established, they generate backward linkages through an extensive demand for component parts, which will probably at first be imported; but these may soon be in sufficient demand to justify the establishment of enterprises to manufacture them domestically. At the same time, if the establishment of the automobile industry results in more cars and trucks being available in the national economy, as will probably be the case, this will cause so-called forward linkages through a greater demand for gasoline and replacement parts, which demand may grow to a size justifying the establishment of industries to make them locally; and this demand will also generate a greater need for garages and for more or less skilled mechanics to operate them.

Advantages of Import Substitution

The import substitution strategy has certain advantages. For one thing, it tends to make the process of industrialization move from the simpler type of manufacturing firm to the more complex, from that requiring relatively limited capital investment, entrepreneurship, and labor sophistication, to that requiring heavier capital equipment, more intricate managerial skill, and more highly trained labor. This is because at the beginning of the import substitution phase, most imports consist of consumer goods, such as textiles, clothing, shoes, or processed foodstuffs, and of light metallurgical products for construction, maintenance, and repair of vehicles and the like. Generally speaking, industries producing these goods are less demanding in terms of capital, entrepreneurship, and labor inputs than are heavier industries. By the time the import substitution process reaches the point of the establishment of heavy industries, the developing country is likely to be in a better position to provide these requirements for itself or to mobilize them abroad than it would have been at the very beginning of industrialization.

This sequence of development is exactly the reverse of that in what we have called the "Soviet" strategy. In a welfare sense, it means that the import substitution strategy does not require—as does the Soviet one—a massive restriction of consumption during the initial phase of industrialization. Quite the contrary, the continuation of the import substitution process requires the maintenance of preexisting levels of consumption and tends to some degree to bring new consumers into the market, as well as to expand the economy's ability to meet their demands.

Another advantage of the import substitution process is the fact that it reduces to secondary importance a wide range of problems which under other circumstances might be serious impediments to development. Because of the existence of a captive market, the fact that costs of production are high during the period of the establishment of industry does not serve to hamper the growth of industry. Increased costs can be passed on to the consumer, who has little alternative but to pay them, or not to consume at all.

Thus, the fact that management is relatively inefficient (as is almost certain to be the case) during the import substitution period, and therefore contributes to high unit costs of output, need not be a matter of primary concern. The fact that it takes a considerable time to develop an efficient and highly productive labor force is also not an immediate drawback to the spread of industry. The fact that costs of obtaining financial capital are very high is also something which can be tolerated for a considerable period.

Somewhat the same thing can be said about the problem of the quality of output. Since consumers generally have no alternative source of supply to that of national industry, they are often forced to put up with a quality of output which is inferior to what might exist under other circumstances. The new entrepreneurs are not immediately forced to deal with problems of quality control, which often demand relatively advanced techniques and training.

The import substitution strategy of development also makes it unnecessary to deal immediately with social problems which under other circumstances might be of major political and economic importance. Thus it is possible for industry to grow up during the import substitution period alongside of an agriculture which is keeping large parts of the population out of the market for manufactured goods and is increasingly unable to meet the growing national need for foodstuffs and agricultural raw materials, without there developing a major clash between the industrial sector and the retrograde agriculture segment of the economy and society. This is because augmentation of the market is not a problem for industry during the import substitution period; and because the process of import substitution makes available foreign exchange which can be used to buy abroad the food and raw materials which are needed but not supplied by national agriculture.[2]

Thus the import substitution strategy of development makes it possible to establish a viable priority list for the use of scarce resources during the early phases of industrialization. In Chapter 4 we go into more detail with regard to this ordering of priorities.

Trends of Exports and Imports

The process of import substitution does not mean, of course, that the total amount of exports will decline. In view of the existence of considerable unemployment of resources, including manpower, which is characteristic of most underdeveloped countries, there will be no need to divert resources from the export industries in order to develop a manufacturing sector. Hence, if the productiveness of the country's major export industries is maintained and its principal customers remain willing and able to purchase the output of these export industries, total quantity and income from exports will remain at or above their previous level. As a result, the industrializing nation should continue to be able to import goods of at least the same value as before the process of industrialization began, and since import substitution in one sector of the economy will usually generate new demands for imports by another sector, the total value of goods and services bought abroad should remain high.

However, during the import substitution phase of development, at least two trends will occur. In the first place, the nature of the nation's imports will change. In the second, the total importance of imports in the overall economy will be likely to decline.

The Economic Commission for Latin America, drawing

upon the experience of the countries within its jurisdiction, which in general are farther advanced along the process of import substitution industrialization than the other developing areas, has described these two tendencies in that region in its publication *The Process of Industrial Development in Latin America*. With regard to the shift in the components of the import sector, this study notes:

> The import coefficient for consumer goods shows a clearly marked downward trend, and reaches the lowest levels, with an average of slightly more than 3 per cent in recent years, of which more than two-thirds corresponds to durable consumer goods (including some types of motor vehicles); moreover, while for some groups of countries it barely exceeds 2 per cent, in one category—comprising the Central American and Caribbean countries—it is even higher than 10 per cent. The relation between imports of capital goods and total fixed investment significantly decreased in certain groups of countries between 1948–49 and 1960, in particular because of the contraction in respect of building materials, but the average coefficient shown is still quite high, namely, a little over 25 per cent, the main components being imports of machinery and equipment. Lastly, in the region as a whole the coefficient of imports of raw materials, intermediate products and fuels, of which the last-named continue to represent a significant proportion, has followed a trend towards stabilization at levels fluctuating between 5 and 6 per cent of the gross domestic product.[3]

The effect of import substitution on the relationship of imports to the total economy has varied widely in the different Latin American countries. However, the ECLA report comments on this as follows:

> The range of different situations is thus sufficiently wide to make it difficult to generalize with respect to Latin America as a whole. Nevertheless, the dominant feature is a substantial long-term decline in over-all import coefficients; and furthermore—a point of basic importance, particularly for the

purposes of defining a future development strategy—the average coefficients registered today, and especially, therefore, the figures for some individual countries, have dropped to levels lower than those recorded in most of the other regions of the world.[4]

A bit further on, the report adds:

Hitherto, the import substitution process has been viewed mainly from the angle of the decrease in the over-all import coefficient. By definition, substitution does not necessarily entail a contraction in the absolute volume of imports, but simply means that they increase more slowly than the total product. With few exceptions, this has been the general characteristic of the process in Latin America. . . .[5]

Post-Import Substitution Crisis

The possibilities of import substitution, however, have their limit. When a country has developed all feasible industries for substitution for imports, this process can no longer serve as the "engine of development." At this point, if further growth of the economy is to take place, it becomes necessary to expand the available markets, either domestic or foreign or both. When productive capacity is equal to the effective demand for most manufactured goods, competition among various firms in a given industry becomes acute. The relatively high costs of production become of importance to the various firms, since one method of expanding the market of each individual firm is to be able to sell at lower prices, thus reaching potential customers who could not afford to pay the previously high costs or taking customers away from rival enterprises. Rationalization of both management and labor, therefore, assumes an importance it did not have previously. Likewise, it is no longer possible to allow agriculture to lag drastically behind the development of industry, since it is now of major importance to the urban sector to get the workers in the rural economy to become purchasers of manufactured goods and to have agriculture become able to provide the raw materials and foodstuffs which are technically feasible in the particular country.

At this point, the society of the developing nation is faced with the need for fundamental reforms of various kinds. Extension of general education and vocational training, the development of a highly efficient managerial force, perfection of capital markets, changes in land tenure, shifts in government investment priorities, and perhaps even basic political reforms become of first-rank importance. This third phase of development—after the growth of export industries and the stimulation of manufacturing through import substitution—is thus in many ways the most difficult aspect of the whole development process. It is the period in which entrenched interests are likely to be most severely hurt, shifts of political power are most drastic, and old ways of doing things have to be changed most radically.

A Rebuttal

As we noted in the Introduction, many economists who have written about economic development have paid relatively little attention to the process of import substitution. However, Gerald M. Meier, in his volume *The International Economics of Development,* has sought at some length to argue against the import substitution strategy of development. We shall try here to rebut some of his major arguments.

Professor Meier has made four principal arguments against import substitution. The first is that the process of import substitution has tended to hamper export industries of the developing country by raising "prices for industrial outputs for agriculture," price controls on agricultural production, neglect of investment in agriculture, and diversion of resources into import substitution.

In response to this it may be said that it is highly debatable that the major difficulties of the export industries of the underdeveloped countries have arisen from the process of import substitution. As Raul Prebisch has pointed out, the ability of the underdeveloped countries to export is principally determined by the willingness of the industrialized countries to buy the export products of the developing nations.

The degree to which this is the case can be demonstrated by noting quickly the situation facing the exporters of some of the principal exports of the developing nations. In the case of coffee, which is a major element in the foreign trade of fourteen Latin American countries and a sizable number of African ones, the limits of expansion of a given country's sales on the world market are fixed by the quota decisions of the International Coffee Agreement, which seek to equate the relatively slowly growing demand of the highly developed countries with the great ability of the underdeveloped ones to provide a large supply. In the case of sugar, the purchase of most of the world's output is determined by decisions of the United States, British, and Soviet governments, and that portion of world production which is sold in the so-called international market, has in many years sold for a price below the cost of production in virtually all of the producing countries.

In the case of bananas, the prices and amounts of product bought are determined largely by a few major importers in the United States, Britain, and continental Europe, which have much more to say about whether a new country can come into the market, or an old producer increase its share of the market than does any government of a producing country. In the case of tin, the amount that a given producing nation can sell is established in accordance with the decisions of the International Tin Council. In the case of copper, the prices paid and amounts bought are largely determined by a handful of large companies which until recently owned all or part of the producing facilities in the various underdeveloped countries, and which still seek to balance their purchases among various regions of the world. Chile, the only seller of natural nitrates, has its market severely limited by the competition of synthetic nitrates. Until recently iron ore was not a major product purchased from the underdeveloped countries, but since World War Two, sources have been opened up in Latin America and Africa by three or four United States steel companies, and the amount that these underdeveloped countries can sell is determined by the needs of the particular United States companies and their desire to "balance" their sources of supply among nations on various continents.

The second major argument of Professor Meier is that tariffs designed to encourage import substitution industrialization will hurt economic development if they merely divert consumption from imports to import substitutions, without stimulating domestic savings and investments. In this case, "home consumption simply rises at the expense of domestic investment, and the imports of capital goods are offset by the reduced domestic investment, so that there is no increase in total net capital formation."

It seems to us that this argument against import substitution is largely a straw man. Import substitution industrialization has in fact involved a great deal of domestic private and public savings and investment, as well as some foreign investment. It has been estimated, for instance, that in Latin America some 90 percent or more of the investment since the early 1960s has been from domestic sources in the Latin American countries.

It is our observation that insofar as the Latin American countries are concerned, at least, the industrialist class is drawn largely from the classes of artisans and merchants, who build up their enterprises from small workshops or stores, by ploughing back their profits into the business. It is unlikely that these elements would be interested in investing extensively in agricultural enterprises. Nor is it likely that foreign manufacturing enterprises who have provided a fair proportion of the capital for Latin American import substitution industrialization would have gone to those countries to grow sugar, bananas, or coffee.

In addition, of course, governments have invested heavily in manufacturing enterprises and in infrastructure designed to support and complement them. Finally, as Albert Hirschman has noted, the problem in most underdeveloped countries is that of bringing latent savings out of hiding, diverting savings from unproductive uses, and providing incentives for more savings. Import substitution industrialization, with its markets, serves all of these functions.

Professor Meier makes two arguments in favor of agricultural development in preference to import substitution industrialization. He maintains that the existence of underemployment in agriculture, which is a major justification for industrialization, is highly questionable. He says that any transfer of labor from agriculture to industry is likely to result in a decrease in agricultural output, unless there are extensive capitalization of the rural sector and extensive changes in social and political institutions, to make it possible to offset the loss of output due to workers being transferred to industry. He also argues that agricultural development is preferable to import substitution because the marginal return from investments in agriculture may well be greater than that arising from import substitution industries.

However, even if one concedes for purposes of argument that underemployment, in terms of the removal of some agricultural workers resulting in a decrease of rural output, is only occasionally encountered in the developing countries—a proposition which Professor Meier by no means proves—this would be largely irrelevant. The fact is that the ability of any underdeveloped nation to develop its economy through augmenting its export of agricultural products is severely limited because of the inelastic demand for these goods in the highly industrialized nations. Professor Meier is the best witness to this, when he states:

> Extreme pessimism characterizes the developing countries'
> outlook for their traditional primary product exports. In spite
> of the rapid economic expansion in the industrial countries

during the postwar period, the growth in exports of foodstuffs and industrial raw materials from the less developed countries to the industrial nations has been disappointingly low. From 1950 to 1965, gross world exports increased by 130 percent, but exports from developing countries rose by only 50 percent; and instead of being nearly one-third of total world exports, as in 1950, the share of developing countries' exports was only one-fifth in 1965. . . .[6]

The ability to expand the economy through expansion of the sector of agriculture destined to grow goods for the national market is strictly limited by the ability to bring about needed changes in rural institutions, particularly in land tenure. This ability is restricted by social and political factors, particularly the power of the traditional landholding class which resists such changes, a power which can be broken only when the strength of the urban-industrial sector is greatly augmented.

In any case, Meier's skepticism about underemployment in agriculture in the underdeveloped countries seems of doubtful validity. In Latin America for two generations there has been massive migration from rural to urban areas without any decline in agricultural output. The slow growth of agricultural production has been due largely to the technologically backward nature of domestically oriented agriculture rather than to a lack of sufficient labor force.

The capitalization and modernization of the segment of agriculture oriented toward the national market require imports of agricultural machinery, fertilizers, insecticides, etc. These imports will constitute a severe burden on the nation's balance of payments, and the increase in agricultural output resulting from this investment will do little or nothing to relieve the burden on foreign exchange. The improvement of the rural sector is likely to be achieved at much less overall cost to the national economy once such a country is at least partly self-sufficient in the manufacture of some of these agricultural inputs.

All of Meier's arguments tend to overlook the fact that through import substitution industrialization the people of a country can have more goods and services at their disposal than they could have without such development. Since the limits to imports are set by the ability to expand exports, which in turn depends basically on the willingness of the great industrial nations to buy, the ability of the people of the underdeveloped country to have consumer goods in the period before industrialization begins is limited by their nation's ability to export. If domestic industries can provide a certain proportion of these goods, the foreign exchange formerly used to import them can be used to bring in goods not formerly available to the economy of the underdeveloped country.

Also implicit in Meier's argument is the idea that protection, which is needed for a nation to undergo import substitution industrialization, will decrease the country's total trade. This is by no means the case. Again, the volume of an underdeveloped nation's foreign trade is determined fundamentally by the willingness of its highly industrialized trading partners to purchase its principal exports. The potential demand of the developing countries for the products of the developed ones is virtually unlimited in the foreseeable future. Certainly there are few if any underdeveloped countries, with the exception of a handful of oil-producing nations, which "hoard" foreign exchange. On the contrary, most of them have a more or less severe and chronic shortage of foreign currency. Hence, in place of the imports for which substitutes are being produced as the result of tariff or other protection, such a nation will purchase other goods; it will not hoard its dollars, pounds, francs, or marks. The total amount of goods and services available to the population of the developing country will be greater than before the beginning of the import substitution process. The goods exchanged in international trade will change as the result of import substitution industrialization, but their total volume will not decrease.

Conclusion

In the chapters which follow, we shall explore various aspects of the import substitution strategy. We shall look in some detail at the prerequisites for the use of this method of development and discuss the priorities for private and public investment during the import substitution phase. Finally, we shall survey details of the problems of the post-import substitution phase.

NOTES

1. Stephen Enke, *The Economics for Development* (Englewood Cliffs, N.J.: Prentice-Hall, 1963), p. 126.

2. Sometimes even economists who are generally sympathetic to the process of import substitution do not recognize the factors which permit a comparative lack of agricultural development during the import substitution phase. Thus in his book *The Theory of Economic Growth*, W. Arthur Lewis lays great stress on the need for "balanced development," meaning the parallel development of agriculture and industry. In his later book *Development Planning* (New York: Harper & Row, 1966, p. 43), he comments in a similar vein: " . . . Since the Second World War most countries have progressed rapidly along the path of import substitution, confining themselves, unfortunately, mainly to manufactures, while tending to ignore raw materials and food. Annual rates of increase of industrial production of 8 to 10 percent have become quite common, in countries where agricultural output increases only by 3 percent or less. . . ."

3. Economic Commission for Latin America, *The Process of Industrial Development in Latin America* (New York: United Nations, 1966), p. 28.

4. *Ibid.*, p, 26.

5. *Ibid.*, p. 27.

6. Gerald M. Meier, *The International Economics of Development* (New York: Harper & Row, 1968), p. 252.

CHAPTER THREE

Prerequisites for an Import Substitution Strategy of Development

There are two essential prerequisites which a country must have if it is to use the import substitution strategy of economic development. One of these is so obvious that it might be overlooked: a country must have a sizable body of imports if it is to industrialize by creating enterprises which make goods to take the place of those imports. The second prerequisite is that the government should follow a policy of providing protection to national industries.

Imports Require Exports

Imports must be paid for by exports. A country cannot buy sizable quantities of goods and services from other nations if it doesn't have something to give its trading partners in return.

Hence, import substitution is of necessity the second stage rather than the first step in any country's process of evolution from an underdeveloped economy to a developed and diversified one. Import substitution is possible only after a nation has entered the world market, selling one or more products which earn it enough income so that it can begin to purchase on a substantial scale goods produced in other countries.

The characteristic pattern, starting from the second half of the nineteenth century, was for most of the nations of Latin America, Asia, and Africa to begin to produce some agricultural or mining commodity which was in demand in the already industrialized nations. This entry into the world market constituted the first phase in the evolution of these nations from countries with largely self-sufficient agricultural economies.

The initiative for this first step in economic development originated in the already industrialized nations. They experienced a rising demand for foodstuffs which they could not meet within their own borders; they lacked within their own frontiers sufficient quantities of the minerals which were essential to a modern industrial economy. Also, lying in the northern part of the Northern Hemisphere, they were unable to produce the tropical agricultural products which were also required to an increasing degree by their economies.

We are all familiar with the nature of the exports from the underdeveloped countries, and whence they came. Gerald Meier and Robert Baldwin, in their volume *Economic Development: Theory, History, Policy,* have shown the spectacular quality of the growth of these exports since the first decade of the twentieth century:

> Examples are many: rubber output in Malaya was only 200 tons in 1905, but by 1920 exports of rubber amounted to 196,000 tons; cocoa production in the Gold Coast and Nigeria increased over 40 times from 1905 to 1939; the total value of Burma's exports, covering years of high and low prices, rose at a rate of 5 percent per annum from 1870 to the 1930's; palm oil exports from the Netherlands East Indies, Malaya and Belgian Congo were only 23,000 tons in 1923, but 305,000 tons in 1937; coffee exports from French West Africa amounted to

6300 tons in 1936, but to 40,000 tons in 1948; cotton exports from French Equatorial Africa rose from 93 tons in 1926 to 27,000 tons in 1948; and so on for copper from Northern Rhodesia, cane sugar from West Indies, tea from Ceylon, etc.[1]

In return for these exports of raw materials and foodstuffs the underdeveloped countries earned sizable quantities of foreign exchange—pounds sterling, dollars, francs, marks. With this income they began to purchase the goods which they generally did not make at home, or at least did not make in sufficient quantities to meet the growing demand of those parts of the population which were being brought into the market by the growth of the export sector.

These goods were generally manufactured products. Before the development of large-scale exports, manufacturing in most of these countries was largely on the basis of handicraft production. This artisan sector of the economy was able to meet the needs of the small urban centers which existed in the preexport period, but was unable to meet the rising demand which appeared once the export industries developed. Nor was it generally able to compete with the wave of cheap manufactured imports which began to come in from the highly industrialized countries.

Impact of Growth of Export Sector

P. J. Bauer has emphasized the importance of the growth of the basic commodity export trade in the development process in the currently underdeveloped countries.[2] In global terms, its impact was to establish alongside the traditional largely subsistence, semimarket economy a new and modern sector which was closely tied to the world market.

Generally, the mines and plantations which were opened up to supply the export markets differed qualitatively from traditional mining and agricultural enterprises. They were modern business firms instead of being a "way of life." They involved very sizable investments of capital in equipment, buildings, health services, and other overhead. They were cost-conscious, since they were in competition with enterprises from other parts of the globe for their share of the world market, and hence sought to rationalize production. They were quality-conscious for the same reason.

Perhaps even more revolutionary from the point of view of the preexisting economy in these countries, these enterprises paid money wages. They generally did not use forced labor—although an exception to this rule might be some of the African mining enterprises. But even these paid money wages to workers forced to work in them. They frequently sought to use wage incentives as an instrument for stimulating production and controlling quality.

In addition, these mining and agricultural enterprises made it necessary to create a great deal of social capital in the countries in which they were established. In order to get the goods to a port from which they could be shipped to the industrial nations, it was necessary to build modern transportation facilities—usually railroads. In order to handle large cargoes adequately, it was necessary to rebuild ancient ports along modern lines, or to create entirely new ones.

In the cities which grew up or expanded as *entrepôts* for this export traffic, it was also necessary to build a great deal of social capital. Sewer and water systems, street lighting, and paved streets became necessities. It was also indispensable to establish commercial enterprises which could handle this trade as well as a banking system which could provide it with credit.

At the same time, the role of the government in these countries began to expand. Instead of being merely a policeman and a postman, the government had to take upon itself new duties. It participated in, or at least authorized, the establishment of many of the transportation facilities and public utilities which were developed. As a result of the growing import-export trade, government revenue markedly increased, while at the same time new demands were made on it in the fields of education and public health.

As a result of all this proliferation of economic activities, a much larger part of the population was brought into the market. Previously, most people had been subsistence farmers, growing enough for their own needs, with perhaps a small margin for sale (or more likely for barter) in the nearest town, and making much of their own housing, clothing, and other needs. Or they were artisans who also bartered at least some of their production for the goods and services they needed.

But now the mines, plantations, railroads, ports, public utilities, expanded government services, commerical houses, banks, all paid money wages and salaries. With these wages and salaries, the people had to pay for their housing, food, clothing, indeed for everything they required for their daily living.

As a result of this expansion of money income in the economy, there came into existence a much larger market than had existed previously, for a wide range of goods, particularly manufactured goods. These items were for the most part not produced in adequate numbers at home, but the expanded import trade— which resulted from the growth of exports—was able to supply them in increasing quantities.

Of course, it was this growth of an internal market which paved the way for any program of further development, particularly one which involved import substitution. It created the market for manufactured goods, which in the first phase of development was supplied by goods from other countries, and in a later period could be supplied by commodities manufactured at home.

In his book *Development Planning,* W. Arthur Lewis has summed up the impact of the development of exports on the internal economy of an underdeveloped country in the following terms:

Productive capacity is increased because these incomes support considerable improvement of infrastructure and of skills, whose benefits are not confined to the products which pay for them. Capital is invested in transportation (harbors, roads, railways, telecommunications), in electric power, in banking and commercial institutions, and in public services (schools, hospitals, water supplies and general administration). The community requires a new set of resources and skills which would serve it to produce new commodities even if the original exports disappeared. . . .

The proceeds of exports are used to buy imports. Thus import substitution becomes a challenge to domestic producers. . . .[3]

Ties to the World Market

This development of the export-import trade tied the presently underdeveloped countries more closely to the world market than they had ever been before. The prosperity of the whole market-oriented segment of the population came to depend upon the country's ability to sell its one or two major export products. If for some reason or other the foreign demand for these products was curtailed, the result was unemployment, lower wages, and other deprivation for those employed in the mines or plantations producing the export commodities. It resulted also in less use of the railroads, ports, commercial houses, banks, and all other institutions connected with the monetized part of the economy. It also brought about a decline in the revenues of the government, which depended more or less heavily on incomes from the export-import sectors.

This influence of the world market was felt all the more drastically because in most cases the countries depended almost exclusively on the export of one, or at most a small range of products. Anywhere from 50 percent to 95 percent of a country's export earnings were likely to come from a single commodity. In addition, the number of trading partners was usually sharply limited. Virtually all of the major export was sold to a handful of industrialized countries.

Hence, a relatively slight dip in the economy of a major industrial nation could bring virtual disaster to one of the raw material or foodstuff exporting countries. Furthermore, the continued expansion of the exporting country came to depend upon the expanding demand of a few industrial nations for these agricultural and mining products.

W. Arthur Lewis has indicated some of the dangers of this phase of a country's economic development:

> Once having started with some favorable commodity, it is very easy to overspecialize; this is why so many countries pass through a stage of monoculture. Specialization pays; it is the secret of economic success. So all the resources associated with the new export tend to specialize in its requirements. Transport is designed to serve it, geographically. Banks, commodity exchanges, legal contracts, research institutes, training facilities, universities and practically everything else, specialize in the problems of this one export commodity, to the neglect of most other opportunities. The community maximizes its gain from this commodity, at the expense not merely of other potential gain, but also of becoming dependent on a market which may easily disappear for reasons beyond its control. [4]

The dangers of overspecialization of their economies became very obvious to the underdeveloped countries during the First World War, the Great Depression, and the Second World War, when they found it very difficult to dispose of their major exports or to buy the manufactured goods which they were accustomed to importing, or both. It was these three events, particularly the Depression, which set in motion the process of import substitution industrialization in much of the underdeveloped world, particularly Latin America. At first, import substitution was begun with little encouragement from the governments concerned, but behind a temporary protective barrier provided by the underdeveloped nations' inability to earn sufficient foreign exchange to purchase their customary imports, or to be able to use the foreign exchange which they did earn.

Growth of Nationalism

All of these developments acted as a spur to the growth of a more or less widespread feeling of nationalism in the underdeveloped countries. Two things, in particular, spurred this growth of nationalism: the feeling of overwhelming dependence upon foreign countries arising from the new dependence on the world market; and the development of classes in these societies which could respond to a nationalistic appeal.

As a result of the dependence of each individual underdeveloped country on the willingness and ability of a particular industrialized nation to buy its principal export, those people of nationalistic tendencies in the underdeveloped country had a "culprit" whom they could blame if the demand for their country's major export product fell off. Even more important, the fact that foreign enterprises—more often than not from the same country which was the nation's principal trading partner—controlled their principal mines or plantations, railroads, gas and electric companies, streetcar lines, major banks, and sometimes ports, became increasingly galling to the nationals of the undeveloped countries.

Nationalistic tendencies were stimulated further by the belief—certainly not without foundation—that the great economic dependence of particular underdeveloped countries on specific industrialized ones seriously limited the effective political independence of the underdeveloped nation. It came to be widely assumed that by subtle or not so subtle economic pressure, a powerful industrial nation could force an unindustrialized one which depended upon it to buy its major export product, to conform to the industrialized nation's desires in the political realm.[5] Futhermore, those entrepreneurial interests in the underdeveloped country which were closely tied to the export trade—the coffee growers of several Latin American countries, the wheat and meat producers of Argentina, to cite but two cases—lived in more or less perpetual fear of reprisals against their businesses if their governments did not conform to the wishes of the major purchaser of their products. They, therefore, brought considerable and constant pressure on their governments to make them so conform.

All of these factors contributed toward the growth of nationalism among elements which were concerned about the sovereignty of their respective nations. They were given new importance by the development of new classes in the societies of the underdeveloped countries and these classes were peculiarly susceptible to a nationalistic appeal. Their growth, in turn, was the direct result of the growth of the export-import economy.

As a result of the expansion of the monetized sector of the economies of these nations, there came into existence sizable middle-class entrepreneurial groups. These included merchants involved in handling exports and imports, the first beginnings of a class of industrial entrepreneurs, and a growing group of artisans.

At the same time, there also grew a much larger class of wage and salaried workers. These included workers in the mines and plantations, in commercial enterprises, and on the railroads. They included also members of the expanded government bureaucracy, among whom perhaps teachers were of particular political significance.

In many countries these middle groups in the society were to a certain degree without deep roots in the society. Many middle-class people were drawn from immigrant groups, or from minority groups which were not quite accepted in the society in which they lived. In other instances, they were people of mixed blood, having forebears drawn from several racial groups, but with strict loyalties to none of them, and thus uprooted from the traditional society which still dominated the nonmonetized sector of the economy.

Without the development of these groups, nationalism, in terms of a popular movement drawing support from broad segments of the community, was virtually impossible. The upper classes tended to be "international" in a sense, taking as their models the societies of Europe and the United States, and feeling more in common with people of those countries than with their own fellow countrymen. At the same time, the traditional lower classes were exceedingly parochial, the limits of their horizons not spreading much farther than the plantation on which they were born or the village in which they grew up. Nationalism could have little real meaning for either of these groups.

However, it had vital meaning to the new groups developed as a result of the growth of the export-import economy. Cut off as they were from the traditional society, socially somewhere in between the traditional ruling groups and the traditional lower classes, they were seeking something around which to center their loyalties. The concept of the nation provided just this kind of a symbol. Hence, it was among these middle segments of the societies of the underdeveloped countries that nationalism first tended to take root.

Nationalism has played a major role in the movement of the underdeveloped nations from the first phase of development based on the export-import sector to development based on industrialization. In the politically independent countries, the intensification of nationalism in the decades after the First World War served to mobilize support behind a program of industrialization, designed to make these countries "economically independent" of (in actual practice, somewhat less dependent on) the highly industrialized powers. In the colonial areas which largely received their independence after World War Two, the desire to get away from what was conceived to be (and often was) too close economic association with the "mother country" was an inherent part of the decolonization drive which ultimately resulted in the attainment of formal political sovereignty.[6]

Imports as Prerequisite for Import Substitution Strategy

The growth of imports is, therefore, essential if a nation is to follow an import substitution strategy of development and industrialization. To have imports, exports are first necessary to provide the foreign exchange with which to pay for imports. This fact has meant that in most of today's underdeveloped countries, the growth of a major industry has constituted the first phase in the process of economic development. It has created the potential market for national industry. At the same time, it has brought into existence social groups which foster the taking of the next step toward industrialization and the development of a more diversified economy.

Need for Foreign Exchange during Import Substitution Period

Imports and exports are not only of first-rate importance as means by which a nation can obtain its first impulse toward economic development. They also are a crucial instrument in carrying a country through its phase of industrialization and economic diversification. This is particularly the case when a nation industrializes through the import substitution strategy.

During the process of industrialization there is extensive demand for the importation of capital equipment to equip new factories and other installations. There is also an extensive need to employ foreign managerial and technical talent, which must be paid in foreign currencies.

In addition, the import substitution strategy presumes that relatively little emphasis will be placed on agriculture. As a result, the rural sector is not able to keep up with the needs of the cities. Therefore, there is a growing need during this period for foreign exchange with which to purchase raw materials for the expanding industries and foodstuffs for the growing population. The rapid increase in their inhabitants, which characterizes most developing countries, and their booming urbanization make this need all the more urgent.

Need for Price Stabilization for Basic Commodities

Because of this continued need for imports and hence the need for maintaining a high level of export income, political leaders and economists from the underdeveloped countries have been strongly insistent on the need for stabilizing the demand for and prices of the key export commodities of the developing countries. They have insisted since World War Two on the need for international agreements to this end.

There has been extensive controversy among economists concerning whether or not the exporters of the major mineral and agricultural commodities are faced with deteriorating terms of trade. A number of economists from developing nations, headed by Raul Prebisch, longtime Executive Secretary of the Economic Commission for Latin America, have insisted that there is a long-range tendency for the prices of these exports to fall, relative to the prices of industrial commodities. This argument has been disputed by many economists of the industrial countries.

Whatever the truth in this controversy—which depends largely on what base date one takes for calculating price changes—it is certainly the case that basic mineral and agricultural exports are subject to much more rapid, frequent, and extreme changes in price than are manufactured goods. It is also apparent that for long periods the tendency of exports of basic commodities to grow has not been as great as the tendency for exports of industrial products to expand.

These facts interfere seriously with the possibility of planning development. Because the governments of the developing countries have little control over their nations' export income and find it very difficult to estimate accurately the amount of foreign exchange that will be available for purchasing capital equipment and other goods required by their economies, they find it exceedingly difficult to establish consistent investment programs.

To some degree, governments have sought to offset unstable export income by obtaining financing for their development programs from international lending institutions and private foreign investors. However, these are both unpredictable sources of foreign income, and in addition a number of developing countries have reached a foreign debt limit which is about as large as their restricted ability to earn foreign currency (with which to pay interest and amortization) will permit.

Hence, leaders of underdeveloped nations have increasingly insisted that the industrialized countries should join in agreements to insure the basic commodity exporters a high and stable level of income from their products. In some fields, such agreements have been worked out.

For a number of years there has existed an International Tin Council, which has sought to balance demand and supply for that metal. Since the early 1960s, most of the countries producing coffee and the largest coffee-importing nations have belonged to an International Coffee Agreement. Unilateral sugar-purchasing policies of the United States and British governments have brought about conditions somewhat similar to those which might exist under international commodity stabilization accords.

These agreements have been only moderately successful in assuring high and stable prices to the countries producing basic commodities. In most other fields, no serious attempt has been made to stabilize prices. There is very strong opposition in the industrial countries to any such general policy, although since 1963 it has been strongly advocated by the United Nations Conference on Trade and Development (UNCTAD), first headed by Raul Prebisch. The situation dramatized by the oil crisis of 1973–1974 has indicated the possibilities of joint action by primary products exporting countries and has raised the question of whether the demand for many of these products may have outpaced the supply. However, it is too early to assert that the relative prices of primary products have risen permanently in comparison with those of manufactured goods.

Antiexport Sentiment in Developing Countries.

In spite of what seems to be the clear and continuing need for large-scale exports and the resultant foreign currency income, a few developing countries have felt that the way to get away from an excess dependency on exports was to kill the export industries. The policies of the first government of Juan Perón of Argentina (1946–1955) seemed to be designed to seriously restrict the nation's traditional exports, which in fact declined significantly during his period in power.

Ernesto Guevara, who was a leading figure in the early years of the Fidel Castro regime, was much more explicit in his rejection of Cuba's traditional export, sugar. He labeled this crop a "chain" on the country's economy. The Castro regime for the first five years followed policies which were designed to greatly reduce, if not destroy, sugar production. It was not until late 1963 that Castro came to the conclusion that these policies were a mistake and reverted once again to putting primary emphasis on the sugar industry. As we indicate elsewhere, the Cuban regime subsequently went to extreme lengths of revulsion against its earlier policies.

Any developing country which deliberately destroys its ability to earn foreign exchange through its traditional export product undoubtedly is tending to hamper its economy. It is limiting its ability to obtain capital equipment, raw materials, and foodstuffs. It also limits its ability to get foreign financing for key development programs.

In his 1950 report *The Economic Development of Latin America and Its Principal Problems,* Raul Prebisch has underscored the advantages of maintaining exports during the industrialization period. He wrote:

> This does not mean, however, that primary exports must be sacrificed to further industrial development. Exports not only provide the foreign exchange with which to buy the imports necessary for economic development, but their value usually includes a high proportion of land rent, which does not involve any collective cost.[7]

As the industrialization process moves forward, the traditional exports will inevitably become less important in the economy. The foreign sector as a whole will come to constitute a much smaller percentage of the total national product. The country will be able to provide for itself many of the key commodities which it formerly had to import.

In time, too, a developing nation's export products should become much more diversified. At least at the end of the import substitution period it should begin to sell abroad some of the products of its new industries, as well as new raw material and agricultural products which the general economic development process has enabled it to produce. It is interesting to note in this connection the campaign of the United Nations Conference on Trade and Development to convince the older industrial countries to remove restrictions on imports of light manufactured goods coming from the developing nations.

Thus, although the move to make the overall economy of a developing state less dependent than formerly on traditional export products is one of the essential features of a development program, any such country will be ill-advised to seek deliberately to destroy its traditional export sectors. Rather, it will be appropriate for such a country to try to maintain or even expand these, to diversify the markets for them, and to try to diversify its list of exports, and hence to increase its ability to import.

Protectionist Prerequisite for the Import Substitution Strategy

The second prerequisite for the use of an import substitution strategy of development is for a developing nation to follow a policy of protectionism for its new industrial sector. Only through such a policy can a country provide the sheltered market for its manufacturing enterprises which is the key element in such a strategy.

Historical evidence indicates that most countries which have industrialized since Great Britain went through the first Industrial Revolution in the last decades of the eighteenth centry and the first part of the nineteenth, have followed the protectionist road. This was notoriously true of the United States. It was likewise the case with France, Germany, Japan, and other present-day advanced manufacturing nations.

However, in spite of this overwhelming historical testimony concerning what those countries which have succeeded in establishing predominant industrial sectors have actually done, a sizable school of economists has continued to argue in favor of free trade and the "theory of comparative advantage." Even today, many economists from developed countries which did not act as these economists are advising—and a minority of the economists from the underdeveloped nations—are telling the leaders of the developing countries that they should put up no "artificial" barrier to international trade.

The theoretical basis for this policy prescription is the theory of comparative advantage. According to this postulate, first put forward by Adam Smith and elaborated in detail two generations later by John Stuart Mill, each nation should concentrate on the production of that good or those goods which it could produce most efficiently. It should exchange the surpluses of these commodities for those goods which it could make only at higher cost. As a result of such a worldwide diversion of labor each nation would turn out the maximum quantity of products for a given factor input, and through international trade, each country, and all nations as a whole, could obtain the greatest possible quantities of commodities.

Whatever the logical beauty of this theoretical construct, it is of only limited applicability to the developing nations of the latter half of the twentieth century. It does not take into account a number of essential problems which face these countries at the present time.

In the first place, it ignores the problem of the inelasticity of the demand for primary products—the principal commodities which the developing countries offer in international trade—which we have discussed at some length earlier in this book. In ignoring this issue, it does not come to grips with the fact that the developing countries, by concentrating principally on the production of their very limited number of export commodities, may be faced with a situation in which they produce more and more and gain smaller and smaller returns from this production.

The theory of comparative advantage also overlooks the problem of unused natural resources and manpower in the developing countries. It presumes that there is full use of available resources since the argument is that the switch of labor, capital, and/or entrepreneurship from their present uses to an alternative would result in lower overall output. However, the problem often faced in the developing countries is not that of shifting resources from sectors which are of relatively high productivity to those in which productivity is lower, but rather the employment of manpower which is either unemployed or woefully underemployed and making use of natural resources which have been more or less completely unused.

We have touched earlier on the question of whether or not there exists extensive unemployed and underemployed labor in the underdeveloped and developing countries. However, a few additional words may be said on this subject.

The constant drift of population from the countryside to the cities of the developing countries during the last couple of generations, with no visible impact on the output of agriculture in these countries, certainly indicates that there has existed and probably still exists considerable underemployment in the rural areas. In the fast-growing cities, the large number of people engaged in petty retail trade in the streets as well as the substantial numbers still engaged in domestic service bear witness to the existence of underemployment there. In addition, a relatively large number of people are completely unemployed; in a few Latin American countries this proportion is as high as an estimated 20 percent of the total work force. Certainly, no output would be sacrificed (as the theory of comparative advantage would argue) by employing some of these unemployed and underemployed people in manufacturing and allied occupations.

However, labor is by no means the only underused resource in the developing countries. In many of these nations there exist mineral resources and potentially arable agricultural land which under the rules of the theory of comparative advantage and free trade will not be used unless and until there is a demand for them from the world economy as a whole, a demand which may not come for generations. However, these same resources might well be used to supply the needs of a domestic manufacturing sector, if one is brought into existence.

Finally, there are undoubtedly sources of financial capital which remain unused insofar as an underdeveloped country is concerned. We have noted that most underdeveloped nations have untapped sources of savings within their borders. In addition, there are potential financial resources available from foreign manufacturing firms—which are not specialized to invest in the development of mineral or agricultural resources which characterize the preindustrial economy of the underdeveloped countries, but which can be attracted if a nation undertakes a program of developing a manufacturing sector.

The theory of comparative advantage also implicitly assumes that there will be no interference with the channels of world trade and that each country will be able continuously to exchange those goods which it can produce at least cost for those in which it does not have a comparative advantage. However, the experience of the last two generations or more provides ample proof that this assumption is not justified in today's world. Two major wars, and several minor ones, have made it difficult, if not impossible, for the underdeveloped nations to obtain from abroad those manufactured goods upon which they had come to depend. In addition, the Great Depression of the 1930s, generated in the major industrial nations, deprived the underdeveloped countries not only of imported manufactured goods but also of markets for their basic commodity exports.

Finally, although even protagonists of the theory of comparative advantage will normally concede the validity of the "infant industry argument," they tend to underestimate greatly the time span during which such an argument may be valid. Thus the problem which the underdeveloped countries are facing, even with regard to a single industry, is not merely that of gaining time for a new industry to become competitive internationally. Rather it is a question of bringing about a massive change in institutions, customs, ways of thinking, which is likely to be a process spanning a generation, not just a short number of years.

It is undoubtedly true, as the supporters of the theory of comparative advantage would concede, that those establishing a new industry in an underdeveloped nation would find themselves without external economies enjoyed by their counterparts in an industrialized country, and thus will have higher initial costs of production. The new industrialist may well have to supply his own electric power, his own transport facilities and educational plant used by those whom he employs. In addition, the new entrepreneur will not have readily available an adequate pool of trained labor and management personnel and will in all likelihood have to do the complete training job himself. The provision of all these additional goods and services will enter into the cost of the goods which the new industry produces, and the output of this new industry will, therefore, almost inevitably be higher priced than competing goods which might be brought in from abroad.

However, in contradistinction to what is implied by the usual version of the infant industry argument (and certainly by that version acceptable to supporters of free trade), this situation is not something which will be overcome in a short while. The construction of adequate national electric power grids or transportation systems which would provide the industrialist with external economies in these fields may take several decades, at least. The molding of illiterate ex-agricultural workers into a modern industrial labor force is likely to be the work of at least a generation. The training of a modern entrepreneurial and management group may take even longer. Hence, the one major exception usually made to the application of the theory of comparative advantage by advocates of free trade is likely to be of long-term duration.

The long-run nature of the need for protectionism in Latin America is underscored by the Secretariat of the Economic Commission for Latin America in its report to the Inter-American Economic Conference in Rio de Janeiro in 1954, in the following terms:

The protectionist policy required by economic development of the peripheral countries need not damage international trade if such a policy is kept within the limit imposed by the self interest of the developing countries. Recognition of this compatibility of objectives will have great importance in the orientation of international trade policy. From the strict point of view of development, protection is not an exception or transitory necessity, but is a systematic long-term requirement. A trade policy which has a starting point different from this one will hamper economic development or bring with it the need for continuous and difficult adjustments which may be avoided if one fully recognizes this principal. . . .[8]

The classical argument against protectionism holds that protectionism will reduce total volume of world trade. However, this is questionable insofar as the developing countries are concerned. The Secretariat of the Economic Commission for Latin America, in its aforementioned 1954 report, explained why this was the case, in the following passage:

If an industrial center of such world importance as the United States increases its purchases of primary products in the periphery countries, the imports of industrial articles will increase in a complementary manner in such countries, although with certain delay. The increase of imports is, then, a reflexive phenomenon. But if the periphery countries increase in an autonomous form its imports from the center, this would not increase perceptibly its role of primary products in the periphery. The periphery has a passive role, while the center has an active, dynamic role in international trade. The center, with its own rhythm of development and its demand for primary products, influences the rhythm of growth of the peripheral countries; but those cannot positively influence the growth of the center, although in a negative way. . . .

Thus, lacking dynamic action on the capacity of the center to absorb primary products, the peripheral country's own capacity to import depends basically on what the center acquires from the peripheral countries. Said in another way, so long as the center can generate international purchasing power in the periphery, the latter can generate purchasing power in the center.[9]

Protection and Import Substitution

It seems unlikely, therefore, that a presently underdeveloped country will be able to industrialize if its government does not have a policy of extensive protectionism. Of course, the effect of such a policy is to create for the new industrialists of the developing nation a sheltered market, within which they are shielded from competition from manufacturers in the already industrialized countries.

Certainly, the application of a protectionist policy, even by a country using the import substitution strategy, requires certain restraint. It cannot be so rigidly applied as to deprive large segments of the consuming public of goods they are willing and able to buy. Everett Hagen has well summed up other limitations of protectionism in his volume *The Economics of Development:*

> It can be agreed that some degree of protectionism or subsidy is advantageous in any country in the early or intermediate stages of development, to foster a faster rate of industrialization than would otherwise occur, and to foster some industries which might otherwise never become established but are economic if established. And it can be agreed, on the other hand, that, except possibly in the extreme case of a country with large and diverse resources and great talents, too great a degree of protectionism or subsidy has economic costs so high that it is difficult to conceive of balancing advantages. Moreover, in later stages of development the advantages of industrialization are probably gained best by industrial specialization and free trade. In later stages of industrialization, that is, when a country has become able to compete in international markets against other industrial producers, the advantage is clearly on the side of free trade. At an earlier stage, free trade within a customs union of partners with more or less equal industrial ability may be optimum.[10]

It will be advisable for a government to have a variety of protectionist techniques at its disposal. Tariffs, which would make it possible for those who are willing to pay much higher prices for imported goods to continue to meet their wants with commodities brought in from abroad, and would reserve to domestic producers only those customers who were not willing to pay these premium prices, might be advisable in some cases. Exchange controls, which would allow selective imports, might be useful in other cases. A quota system, limiting imports only to that segment of the national market which local producers could not satisfy, might be preferable in still others.

In any case, protectionism makes an import substitution strategy of development possible. It presents the new industrialists with a situation in which they know that they have a market for their products—the market hitherto provided for by imported goods. This means that the principal problem facing the new industrialists is that of finding the ways and means of meeting a demand which is demonstrably present, rather than that faced by their counterparts in the already industrialized countries, of finding a market for their goods and assuring their control over it. For a while at least, there will be a ready-made demand for anything which the producers can turn out, and they have little or no problem of generating new demands.

Thus, once there has come into existence a market for manufactured goods—satisfied in the first phase of development by goods imported from abroad—and this market has been assured to the domestic producers by a protectionist policy, a nation is in a situation to follow an import substitution strategy. As we shall see, this strategy will have certain advantages for the industrialists and for the makers of public policy.

NOTES

1. Gerald M. Meier and Robert E. Baldwin, *Economic Development: Theory, History, Policy* (New York: John Wiley & Sons, 1957), p. 326.

2. P.J. Bauer, *Economic Analysis and Policy in Underdeveloped Countries* (Durham, N.C.: Duke University Press, 1957).

3. W. Arthur Lewis, *Development Planning: The Essentials of Economic Policy* (New York: Harper & Row, 1966), p. 20.

4. *Ibid.*, pp. 41–42.

5. In recent years the experience of Cuba with both the United States and the Soviet Union provides extensive evidence for this argument.

6. It is worth noting, in passing, the importance of nationalism as an entrepreneurial force. In this connection, it is fascinating to note the way in which, as colonies received increased autonomy on the road to independence, their governments began to foment a broad kind of development program mobilizing private as well as fiscal resources, for the development of social capital, industries, and agricultural projects which the colonial governments had usually professed themselves incapable of launching, and which sage economists from the "mother country" often proclaimed to be "impossible."

7. Raul Prebisch, *The Economic Development of Latin America and Its Principal Problems* (Lake Success, N.Y.: United Nations, 1950), p. 6.

8. Economic Commission for Latin America, *La cooperación internacional en la politica de desarrollo latinoamericano* (New York: United Nations, 1954), p. 71.

9. *Ibid.*, pp. 66–67.

10. Everett Hagen, *The Economics of Development* (Homewood, Ill.: Richard D. Irwin, Inc., 1968), p. 463.

CHAPTER FOUR

Development Priorities in the Import Substitution Period

The adoption of the import substitution strategy of development by any nation implies a series of policies which will be followed in various economic fields. It indicates priorities among various sectors of the economy; among the several branches of industry; in entrepreneurial policies; in infrastructure needs; and in the field of labor relations.

Sectoral and Regional Priorities

Import substitution certainly involves emphasis on industrialization rather than on agricultural development. At the beginning of the import substitution process, it is manufactured goods which constitute the great majority of a developing nation's imports, and it follows that it is on the production of these commodities that the country's development efforts will be concentrated.

There are additional reasons why it is advisable to put primary emphasis on the development of manufacturing. A program designed to put priority on the growth of agriculture would involve the need for a great deal of investment in agricultural implements and machinery, fertilizers, and other inputs in this field. Such a program would put very heavy burdens on the nation's balance of payments, without any prospect that when the agricultural development program had been successful the country would be any better able to bear this increased foreign exchange burden.

We have explained elsewhere why an agricultural development program which put primary emphasis on the growth of traditional exports would not be likely to be crowned with any great success in fomenting the general development of the economy. However, a program concentrating on providing agricultural goods for the domestic market would not be any more successful. It would soon be faced with the fact that the cities, lacking manufacturing industries and the incomes which they would generate, would not be able to purchase the rural area's greatly increased output or be able to supply the rural sector with its needs in terms of industrial goods. Nor would agriculture designed for domestic consumption provide the foreign currency needed for its own development or the general growth of the economy.

Furthermore, for an adequate program of agricultural development in many of the underdeveloped countries, it would be necessary to transform the land tenure structure and other aspects of traditional agriculture. However, in order to make such a process possible, it would be necessary for the political power of the cities to grow sufficiently that they could impose upon reluctant traditional landlords an agrarian reform and other needed changes. But growth in the relative power of the cities would not be likely without the growth of industries, which would increase the economic importance and population and hence the political influence of the urban areas.

A certain school of thought among economists (particularly those of the industrialized countries) argues that the underdeveloped countries should seek to have a "balanced" program of development, that is, should seek to push both agriculture and manufacturing. However, the fact is that in underdeveloped countries, the economy is very much "unbalanced" in favor of agriculture, and if balance is a desirable objective of economic policy, it would seem that major attention would have to be paid for a considerable period of time to fomenting manufacturing.

Furthermore, the strategy of import substitution means that so long as import substitution is the "motor force" of development, emphasis on agriculture is not necessary to assure general rapid growth and diversification of the economy. The economy does not face during this period any major crisis as the result of the backwardness of agriculture.

A priori, retrograde agriculture might be assumed to hold back general economic development in two ways. On the one hand, it serves, because of the prevalence of subsistence farming and low productivity, to keep a large percentage of the population out of the market for manufactured goods. On the other, it results in the rural areas not being able to provide the growing quantities of foodstuffs and raw materials which are needed by the urban sector.

However, during the import substitution period neither of these factors is of crisis proportion. Since the problem facing the manufacturers is not that of increasing their markets, but rather one of meeting a demand which was formerly taken care of by imports, the fact that rural workers and subsistence farmers cannot buy the industrialists' products in large quantities is not a matter of immediate concern.

Nor is the failure of agriculture to provide sufficient food and raw materials of pressing importance during the import substitution period. Since foreign exchange which was formerly used to purchase manufactured goods abroad is no longer needed for this purpose, as the result of increasing quantities of these commodities being made at home, growing amounts of foreign currency are available for alternative uses. A certain percentage of this foreign exchange can be used to bring from abroad the foodstuffs and agricultural inputs of industry which might conceivably be grown at home but are not because of the backward state of agriculture.

Another kind of general economic priority which is indicated by the import substitution strategy is the regional concentration of industrialization. There will be a tendency for primary attention in industrialization and general economic development to be concentrated on the national capitals, the principal port cities, and perhaps a handful of other major urban centers.

During the preceding period of development of primary commodity exports, port facilities for handling these exports were developed, and the role of the government in the economy had tended to increase. Hence, there had been considerable expansion of population in the ports and the capital. There had also been a growth of infrastructure and social capital needed to provide basic services for these cities and adequate personnel for all aspects of the export economy.

In the following phase of development, that of import substitution, the major problem will be the growth as rapidly as possible of a manufacturing sector of the economy and the infrastructure and services needed by this new sector. It will be most economical, therefore, for the new industries to be established principally in or near those population centers which are already reasonably well equipped with such things as electric power, public utilities, transportation facilities, housing, schools, and medical services. It is in these centers also that the large part of the national market for manufacturing goods is likely to be found.

As a result, during the import substitution phase there is apt to be a disproportionate degree of development in these favored parts of the national territory. At the same time, the more remote areas of the country will receive relatively little of the new manufacturing enterprises or the infrastructure improvements, and some segments of the nation may feel virtually no impact at all from the industrialization process in this phase.

Priorities in Establishment of Industries

The import substitution strategy of development establishes a logical sequence through which industrialization will proceed. When the serious process of developing manufacturing industry begins, the first enterprises which are established will be those which produce substitutes for the commodities which constitute most of the country's manufactured imports. These are light consumer goods and construction materials, such things as textiles and clothing, shoes, processed foodstuffs, plastics, pharmaceuticals, some light metallurgical products, as well as cement.

The establishment of these industries producing consumer goods and construction materials brings about the importation of machinery for these new branches of production. It thus may create the possibility of a new spurt of import substitution. For instance, if a textile industry is established, there arises an appreciable demand for thread, dyestuffs, sizing, and other inputs into this industry, creating the possibility of establishing firms to make substitutes for these imports. Replacement parts for the textile machinery may be imported in sufficient quantity to justify establishing a plant to manufacture them.

Also, as more firms produce various types of metal products and as the construction industry grows, there begins to be an increase in imports of the products of heavy industry and semiprocessed raw materials, thus extending the import substitution cycle. This means that there may be a sufficient national market to justify the establishment of an integrated iron and steel industry, and heavy chemical production.

Finally, a country which is developing through the import substitution strategy may reach a fourth level of industrialization. Through the growth of heavy industry, the expansion of electric power facilities, and the spread of a road network, a developing country may generate substantial imports of light and even heavy machinery. If these imports are sufficient, there will be a basis for a further phase of import substitution, with the establishment of enterprises producing generators and dynamos, heavy earth-moving and construction equipment, and industrial machinery.

The strategy of import substitution industrialization thus provides a self-expanding process of economic development, by periodically generating new imports, which in turn bring into existence new possibilites for substitution for these imports. It also expands the total market for industrial goods in another way. As new industrial and service enterprises are established, they draw into the ranks of wage earners people who formerly earned little or no money income. Thus people who were not "in the market," that is, who did not earn enough to buy an appreciable amount of manufactured goods, are converted into customers of the nation's new factories. The market, which in the beginning of the industrialization process consisted only of people who had previously purchased imported goods, is thus augmented by others who had previously bought few, if any, factory-made products at all.

Development in Breadth vs. Development in Depth

The import substitution strategy also encourages what the Economic Commission for Latin America has called "development in breadth" as opposed to "development in depth." In ECLA's *Problemas y perspectivas del desarrollo industrial latinoamericano* (p. 35) there is a description of the differences between these two patterns of development and the reasons for the preference for the former:

> In development in depth, most of the annual reinvestment by entrepreneurs is made in their own enterprises, in the form of progressive modernization and consequent reduction in costs.

The proportion of products manufactured in the country does not increase rapidly from year to year, but the efficiency of the existing activities does.

In development in breadth, the most usual type in Latin American industry, profits are usually reinvested in new activities, the production of new items, which can replace those formerly imported, while the existing activities remain at a standstill as regards average productivity. Development in breadth appears to offer more advantages to the private entrepreneur, because in new lines of production, at least for the first few years, competition is very limited and the producer may have a virtual monopoly, whereas reinvestment in the same field continually increases competition, and also because it is easier to establish a wholly new production unit than to keep modernizing and improving existing plants, where routine is strongly entrenched.[1]

One might add that this kind of development in breadth permits the general development of the economy to proceed on a more self-sustained basis, and industrialization to meet a larger segment of the general demand for goods and services more quickly than would be the case with development in depth. It helps to postpone for some time the kinds of crisis in development which, as we shall indicate in the next chapter, are very likely to come when the possibilities of basing development on import substitution have been largely exhausted.

Entrepreneurial Priorities

The import substitution strategy tends to define priorities for the industrial entrepreneur. It indicates to him the major problems he must resolve in the relatively short run and those problems he can put aside for a considerable period of time.

Working with a sheltered market and trying to produce domestically those manufactured products which were formerly imported, the major preoccupations of the industrialists, individually and as a group, are likely to be the accumulation of sufficient capital and learning how to make the best possible use of this capital for production goals. The problem of raising sufficient capital is a very difficult one. In the preindustrial economies of the developing countries there do not exist well-organized capital markets, so that it is difficult, if not impossible, for the industrial entrepreneur to raise his necessary resources by the issuance of stock to "the general public" since the means of reaching this general public virtually do not exist. Furthermore, during much of the early phase of industrialization, the entrepreneur would probably be reluctant to share ownership of his enterprise with "strangers" even if it were possible to do so, since the traditions of the preindustrial economy, which insist upon the individual owning and controlling "his own" property, remain very strong.

Nor is the alternative of bank borrowing as a source of financial capital a feasible one during most of the early period of industrialization. The banking system, such as it is, which has grown up during the first development phase, came into existence largely to finance the movement abroad of the country's principal primary product exports and the bringing in of its manufactured imports. It is essentially a commercial, not an investment, banking system dealing in short-term credit, seldom for more than 180 days. Indeed, the national banking laws of the developing countries frequently forbid the establishment of private investment lending institutions. Although it may be possible in some instances to get around such laws and traditions by a tacit agreement between the banker and the industrial borrower to renew more or less indefinitely ostensibly short-term loans every time they come due, this is an unsatisfactory and dangerous method of financing long-term capital investments.

The industrial entrepreneur will thus have three means available for financing capital accumulations: his own resources, foreign investors, and the government. Not infrequently he will have recourse to all three of these.

The industrial entrepreneur is likely to have commenced his manufacturing activities after having been either a small artisan or a merchant. He has expanded and mechanized his workshop until it has assumed the proportions of a factory; or he has begun to make for himself some of the things which he formerly bought from someone else and sold in his capacity as a merchant. In either case, the enterprise has grown largely by the process of ploughing back profits, and it is likely to continue doing so at least in part after it becomes a manufacturing plant.

The domestic industrialist may also find it useful to form some kind of a partnership with a foreign firm. Such a connection may provide not only financial capital but also access to valuable patents and other forms of technical and managerial know-how. However, from the local industrialist's point of view, it will also have the drawback of limiting the scope of his entrepreneurial authority.

In most countries undergoing import substitution industrialization, foreign investment is not a novelty. Generally, foreign firms and individuals have played a major role in the preindustrialization phase in building up the raw material and foodstuff exports which pave the way for industrialization. Since the fomenting of production of these agricultural and mineral products has usually come about because of the demand for them in the already industrialized nations of Europe and North America, it is perhaps natural that entrepreneurs from those areas would play a key role in investing in these sectors of the economies of the underdeveloped nations. Mineral production, such as copper, tin, lead, zinc, and petroleum, and agricultural output, such as coffee, sugar, bananas, and cacao, have been largely brought about by foreign investors. At the same time, foreign entrepreneurs from the already developed nations have also played a major role in bringing into existence the infrastructure, such as railroads, ports, city improvements, and even electrical power which were essential for the growth of agricultural and mineral exports.

In the import substitution phase it is not only individual industrialists but the governments of the developing countries which will have to deal with the question of foreign investments in their economies. The import substitution strategy, with its emphasis on making the nation able as rapidly as possible to produce those manufactured goods which were formerly imported, would seem to indicate that if foreign firms can help in the process they should be welcome. However, there are other aspects to this problem which do not make this decision quite so clear-cut.

On the one hand, there is the issue of nationalism. The developing countries are generally characterized by widespread feelings of nationalism among their citizenry. There exists, as a result, a widely prevalent fear that foreigners may get an excessive degree of control over the national economy through their investments. This will mean that decisions of great importance to the national economy may be made in the headquarters of these foreign firms, in terms of what is most advantageous to the foreign company involved rather than in terms of what is best for the developing country. There is also fear that foreign enterprises may acquire too great influence in domestic politics and may be able to limit the ability of the national government to follow economic and social policies of its own choosing. Finally, there may even be fear of the implications of an appeal for support by a foreign firm to its own government against policies of the administration of the developing nation.

In addition, there is a strictly economic consideration of some importance when a developing nation's government is deciding whether or not to admit foreign investors. This is the fact that these investors in most cases expect to receive, in the currency of their own country, all or a major part of the returns from their investments in the developing nation. In time such repatriation of profits, and in some cases of capital as well, may come to be a major factor in the developing country's balance of payments and severely limit its possibility to import goods and services which it needs.

Hence, although the import substitution strategy would seem to suggest an encouragement of foreign investment in industrialization, there are certainly countervailing arguments militating in the opposite direction. In many developing countries there seems to have evolved since World War Two a policy pattern on the subject. This pattern provides for nationalization of early investments in the infrastructure made during the period of development through expanding basic commodity exports in conjunction with encouragement of a sizable amount of foreign investment in the manufacturing sector.

A third source of financial capital for the industrial entrepreneur is the government of his country. The strategy of import substitution, with its emphasis on industrialization, involves a commitment from a government following such a strategy to use credit resources available to it to stimulate the accumulation of capital for manufacturing. To this end, many governments of developing countries have established special credit institutions for this purpose, in the form of industrial banks or economic development corporations.

Foreign exchange is as necessary as financial resources in domestic currency for facilitating the accumulation of physical capital during the import substitution phase of economic development. A government committed to an import substitution strategy will be likely to try to direct the expenditure of foreign exchange resources in such a way as to facilitate the importation of necessary capital equipment, as well as raw materials required by the new manufacturing firms. The government development banks and corporations frequently serve a useful function in obtaining and channeling foreign currency loans from foreign governments, international lending institutions, and upon occasion even from private investment banks in the industrialized countries. Exchange controls may be required to set up a system of priorities in the use of foreign exchange being earned through exports of goods and services.

The acquisition of a certain quantity of skilled technical and managerial personnel will also be a high priority need during the import substitution period. Although the import substitution strategy serves to reduce the urgency of having a large stock of such human capital, a new enterprise will certainly require personnel who can organize the firm, deal with its basic technical problems, and thus get it under way and keep it in operation. Self-made entrepreneurs will in most cases not themselves possess the technical knowledge and ability required and will have to employ some native managerial and technical talent if it is available or seek it abroad.

However, just as the import substitution strategy tends to dictate certain high priorities, it also indicates those problems which do not have to be dealt with immediately. It makes it unnecessary for industrial entrepreneurs to concentrate time and attention on certain problems which are of primary importance to their counterparts in the already industrialized nations. These relatively low-priority managerial concerns are the result of the fact that the industrialist is working within a sheltered market, and is not faced with the problem of expanding his market but rather with that of developing the physical capability of providing goods for a market that already exists.

As a result of having a protected market, the industrial entrepreneur is in a position to pass on high costs of production to his customers. Since the buying public has little or no alternative to purchasing the products of the new national manufacturers or doing without these commodities entirely, they will be willing to pay relatively high prices.

Hence it is not a matter of major concern to the industrial entrepreneur during the import substitution period that their costs of labor are relatively high. Although money wages in the developing countries tend to be low in comparison with those in the industrialized nations, productivity of workers also tends to be less than that in the more highly developed economies. In addition, there are other costs of labor which do not appear directly in the wage bill. These may include high payments for social security, funds which have to be kept available for high dismissal payments, and other legal obligations connected with the labor force.

Extra labor costs are also caused by the problem of converting often illiterate, untrained peasants from a backward rural cultural setting into qualified modern industrial workers. It takes time for a new factory worker recruit from the countryside to become accustomed to the idea of working a full eight-hour day, to learn how to live on a money income, to become used to residing in a modern house or apartment, and to become accustomed to factory discipline.

Efforts to convert such workers into a modern industrial labor force involve added costs. Employers have to provide training facilities, housing, medical facilities, and special loan funds for their workers. All these items add to the costs of production of manufacturing in the developing countries.

The possibility of passing added labor costs on to the consumers is perhaps also an element helping to explain another factor in the labor picture in many of the presently developing countries using the import substitution strategy. This is the existence of an extensive and sometimes relatively powerful trade union movement. Since the continuation and growth of production rather than the holding down of costs is the major objective of the industrial entrepreneurs, they may often be willing to make concessions to the unions on questions of wages and fringe benefits which they would not otherwise be willing to make.

The same may be said about the social security systems which are so extensive in the developing countries. These usually provide health insurance, as well as protection against the risks of old age, widowhood, orphanhood, etc. The taxes levied to pay for these social security systems are frequently very high, in comparison with the basic wage rate upon which they are imposed.

Other kinds of labor legislation which are common in the contemporary developing countries also tend to add to labor costs. These include statutes providing for the eight-hour day, protection against the dangers of machinery, minimum wages, vacations with pay, overtime compensation, and similar benefits.

The existence of more or less strong labor movements, as well as of social security systems and extensive labor protection legislation, constitutes a major difference between the conditions of industrialization of presently developing countries and those of nations which went through this process a century or more ago. They are explained in part by the "demonstration effect" of similar institutions and legislation in the major industrial powers and proselytizing by labor movements in these powers. There is little likelihood that any nation which is industrializing at the present moment will do so under circumstances in which there is no organized labor movement, no social security system, or no labor legislation.[2]

The strategy of import substitution may also help to cast some light on a question which is frequently raised in connection with the existence of a trade union movement and extensive labor and social legislation in the currently developing countries: whether the increases in labor costs which unions and labor law cause serve to slow down the process of industrialization and development. During the period of import substitution, it would seem that such is not the case. Since the increased labor costs will not generally serve to force the firms having them to slow down their expansion because of lack of markets during this period, it would seem that unions and labor and social legislation do not serve to slow down the general economic development process.

Just as labor costs do not have to be a major preoccupation of industrialists in developing countries following the import substitution strategy, neither do relatively high managerial costs. Although it is certainly necessary to have sufficient depth of managerial talent to get new industrial enterprises going and to keep them from undergoing major breakdowns, it is not required that management be as efficient as might otherwise be the case. Extensive cost accounting, extensive departmentalization and rationalization of management, a high degree of expertise in the organization of production are not first-priority requirements during the import substitution phase of development.

Another kind of cost which is likely to be much higher in developing countries than in the already developed ones is that of financial capital. Not only are interest rates and returns on invested capital high, but capital markets are usually not organized for the provision of long-term funds to manufacturing enterprises. Rather, the banking system, which has been established during the preindustrial era in which the major export sectors have developed, concentrates on the provision of the kind of short-term credit needed for internal commerce and foreign trade.

However, relatively high costs are not the only type of problem which does not have to be a first-rank source of attention to the industrial entrepreneur in the import substitution period. The same is true of quality. Again, since the customers have little choice but to purchase the output of local industry, they will tend to buy it whether its quality is high or mediocre. Because the market tends to be big enough for all of the limited number of competitors who are generally present during this phase of development without their having to put emphasis on trying to take customers away from one another, competition will not tend to foment improvement of quality. As a result, quality control does not rank high in the priority list of manufacturers during this phase of industrialization.

Finally, industrial firms during this period do not have to put great emphasis on advertising. Since the problem facing the entrepreneurs is not that of expanding the market, but rather that of meeting the demands of a market which already exists, and firms are not primarily concerned with taking customers away from their competitors, they do not feel a great incentive to advertize.

The author has had this problem brought home to him on various occasions in conversations with advertising executives in several developing countries. These people have complained that most of their business comes from foreign firms and that the domestic ones have not "learned the usefulness of advertising."

One might interpret the situation somewhat differently from the way advertising executives tend to do. It might be argued that the foreign firms have merely applied in the developing country policies and techniques which were essential in the industrial nations in which they had their headquarters, whereas the domestic entrepreneurs had not yet experienced a need for extensive use of advertising.

Thus the adoption of the import substitution strategy of economic development implies many other facts about the way in which development will proceed.

Infrastructure Priorities

The import substitution strategy of economic development tends to establish its own logical set of priorities in the fields of infrastructure and social capital. This strategy indicates those transportation and power developments which are of greatest urgency for general economic development. It also tends to define what is most needed, in terms of development, in the fields of education and health.

The problem of priorities is of great importance because of the fact that available resources for infrastructure and social capital development—as for everything else—are very scarce and expensive in a developing country. To the degree that decisions in this area are made on the basis of what is required for economic development, the strategy of import substitution will indicate the appropriate priorities.[3]

Two factors are of underlying importance in determining infrastructure policy. These are the facts that development attention is centered during the import substitution phase on the major cities and, within them, on the manufacturing sector.

In the field of transportation facilities, a different orientation is needed from that which characterized the earlier development period, when major emphasis was being placed on fomenting the nation's raw material and foodstuff exports and those aspects of the economy which served them. During this earlier period, transportation facilities—principally railroads—were built mainly between the mines or agricultural areas producing the major exports and the ports which facilitated the shipping of these export commodities to foreign countries.

Little attention was given to trying to establish a nationwide transportation network, tying together the nation's principal population centers. Argentina is perhaps the prime example of this phenomenon. Virtually all of its railroads, which were constructed largely during the era of development of grain and meat exports, had their termini either at the port of Buenos Aires or at that of Rosario. Almost no railroads connected interior cities with one another, unless these happened to be on the road from meat or grain growing areas to the port cities.

However, during the import substitution phase of development a different transportation policy is required. For one thing, this phase usually has occurred at a time when roads have become a more economical form of transport than the railroads. Second, the need in the import phase is to tie together the principal urban centers in order to assure a national market for the country's new manufacturing establishments. Hence, emphasis during this period will be on the construction of trunk highways, facilitating the transport of goods from the principal manufacturing centers to the main cities and towns of the interior. In some cases, too, existing railroad systems may be extended to connect interior cities.

However, there are certain kinds of transportation facilities whose construction is not of highest priority for economic development during the import substitution period. Since emphasis is not being put in this period upon the development of agriculture, there is no pressing need for the construction of neighborhood and feeder roads to predominantly rural areas, useful mainly for getting agricultural products to main highways, along which they can be shipped to the urban centers.

In the field of power, too, the import substitution strategy dictates certain priorities. The construction of hydroelectric and thermoelectric facilities which can provide adequate and economical power for the new industries is essential. So, too, are facilities for meeting the general power needs of the urban areas, with their rapidly growing population—to keep their transportation and communication networks functioning, to provide street lighting and electricity for the growing number of homes in the cities and towns.

However, in this field, too, there are certain power demands the meeting of which is not necessarily of first priority for the country's continued rapid economic development. Rural electrification, for instance, is not a pressing need during this period. Also, insofar as the development of industry is apt to be geographically concentrated in certain parts of the country during the import substitution period, the establishment of adequate power facilities in those parts of the nation most involved in the industrialization process will be more urgent than their construction in others.

Educational policy is also indicated by the import substitution strategy. The development of industry requires a considerable extension of general literacy among the working-class population; factory workers can do their jobs a great deal better if they can read and write. In addition, industries and the services which they bring into existence require a considerable staff of white-collar personnel whose education goes considerably beyond "the three r's." Finally, there will also be an increasing need for people with a university education to fill managerial posts, the expanding professions, and the growing number of governmental positions.

However, here, too, the extension of educational facilities in some parts of the country will be more urgent than their growth in others. There will be little immediate need for development of educational institutions in the rural areas, and the need for development of schools in the parts of the country in which there is special concentration of industry will be greater than in those where industrialization is proceeding less rapidly.

In some developing countries it may be necessary to begin almost from the beginning, at least insofar as secondary and university educational institutions are concerned. In nations in which universities do not exist—as was the case until a few years ago in most African countries—it will be necessary to create them, as well as to amplify existing secondary schools, in order to create the growing numbers of managers, civil servants, and white-collar workers who will be required as a result of industrialization.

There is also need for the growth of training facilities as well as for those for education. The expanding industries will require increasing numbers of workers with special skills. Although much of this training will be done by the industrial employers themselves, there will undoubtedly also be a growing demand from them as well as from workers who would benefit by such programs, and from the general public, for the government to provide at least some of the schools necessary for training workers to fit into the new manufacturing enterprises.

Finally, there will be a growing demand for a change in the quality of education as well as an increase in its quantity. In most underdeveloped countries in the preindustrial period the educational system was designed for the education of the sons of a small elite. It tended to be "classical," with heavy emphasis on law and the humanities, with little attention paid to the physical and social sciences. On the university level, in particular, it frequently tended to be in the hands of professors whose teaching duties were marginal. The universities were rarely centers of research and of pushing back the frontiers of knowledge.

Such an educational system is not adequate to the needs of a rapidly industrializing society. During the import substitution phase of development, there will undoubtedly be a beginning in the process of transforming the educational system into one which can provide at least elementary schooling for the whole population and can provide the varied kind of training and education which is required by the vastly increased number of specialized jobs generated by a modern industrial society. However, the completion of such a change in the educational establishment will become of primary urgency only in the post-import substitution phase of development.

Investment policies in the field of health and medical services are also largely defined by the import substitution strategy. High on the priority list is certainly control of epidemic diseases, particularly in the urban areas. Also, due to the rapid rise of the urban population, first importance must be given to providing sewer systems, potable water supplies, and hospital facilities for the cities and industrial towns. Finally, since a reasonably healthy labor force is essential for modern industrial enterprises, special programs of medical aid to the industrial workers, through social security systems and through private efforts of industrial entrepreneurs, will be of major importance during the import substitution period.

Again, in this sector as in others, the needs of the rural areas and of outlying parts of the country not heavily involved in the industrialization process will (from the economic development point of view at least) be of distinctly secondary importance. The establishment of rural clinics, the extension of the medical services of social security to the countryside, the building and equipping of hospitals in the smaller cities and towns relatively unaffected by industrialization, will be likely to get scant attention during the import substitution phase of development.

Conclusion

The import substitution strategy presents a rational set of priorities for development. Since resources are limited in the developing countries, and it is impossible for them to do everything at once, these nations need some basis for deciding which projects shall be undertaken first and which can be postponed until a later time. The import substitution process provides such a basis.

NOTES

1. Cited in ECLA, *The Process of Industrial Development in Latin America* (New York: United Nations, 1966), p. 31.

2. For an extensive discussion of these high labor costs in three developing countries, see the author's *Labor Relations in Argentina, Brazil and Chile* (New York: McGraw-Hill, 1962).

3. It might be noted that noneconomic motives and foreign aid may also sometimes influence the determination of infrastructure priorities. Political pressures may be brought to bear on a government to get it to build roads or other public works which are not primarily motivated by considerations of economic development. Foreign technicians may succeed in imposing preconceived notions of what infrastructure projects are most essential, and have the funds to back up their judgment, an argument which it may be hard for the government of an underdeveloped country to resist.

CHAPTER FIVE

The Post-Import
Substitution Crisis

The import substitution strategy has its limits. This is an aspect of the import substitution strategy which its early enthusiasts, such as the economists of the Economic Commision for Latin America, overlooked. The sudden realization of the limits of import substitution has unjustifiably brought some of these early supporters to turn against the import substitution strategy as such.

Every developing nation which is using the import substitution strategy will come to the point at which the process of substitution for imports can no longer function as the "engine of development." This does not mean that a nation has reached a state of autarchy, but only that import substitution can no longer be counted on to provide a more or less automatic continuation and extension of the development process.

The point at which the exhaustion of the import substitution strategy will be reached will be different for each developing country. Such factors as the size of population, the availability of natural resources, the degree to which the population had been involved in the market at the beginning of the import substitution process will determine how far import substitution can carry a nation toward a broad and integrated industrial-agricultural-commercial economy.

At the end of the import substitution phase, the nature of the development problem changes. Whereas during this phase it has been principally one of producing the physical capacity and personnel adequate to turn out the quantity of goods required by an existing market, it now becomes one of expanding the market. If the economy and the individual enterprises within it are to continue to grow, it will be essential to get new customers for the goods and services which the economy can produce.

The critics of import substitution as a strategy of development often, if not usually, do not recognize that import substitution is only applicable during one phase of a country's development toward a diversified, high-income economy. Thus, Harry Johnson, after noting that enterprises from the developed countries which seek to take advantage of the protection provided for new manufacturing firms are likely to bring in techniques and technology which are not appropriate to the economy of a developing nation, comments:

> All this suggests that a policy of import-substitution is unlikely to transform an underdeveloped country into a major industrial power, competitive in the world market for manufactured products. Instead, such a policy is likely to transform it into a miniature replica of the economics of the advanced countries, though less efficient and technologically laggard to an extent depending on the size of the domestic market and the degree of protection employed.[1]

A priori, there are two possible ways of expanding the market as a whole. Either elements of the population which have not participated in the market economy, or have participated in it only slightly, can be brought fully into this economy, or an effort can be made to generate export markets for the goods produced by national industries which hitherto have been sold only within the national boundaries. To a considerable extent the prerequisites for achieving either of these alternatives are the same.

Raul Prebisch, one of the first economists to center attention upon import substitution as a strategy of economic development, has concluded, at least in some of his writings, that at the point of exhaustion of import substitution as the dynamic factor in development, the developing nation's only way out is to obtain markets abroad for some of its manufacturing output. Thus, in his 1963 United Nations monograph *Towards a Dynamic Development Policy for Latin America,* he wrote:

> As long as there was an ample margin of imports which could be dispensed with in the immediate future, or deferred, the expansion of some imports could for the moment be held up or their volume restricted while substitution was being affected in respect of other items. Imports of essential or urgently-needed goods could thus steadily increase without affecting the tempo of internal economic activity. But once this margin narrows or disappears altogether this proceeding cannot be repeated, particularly when the flow of exports is reduced or their volume is contracted, while demand for such imports continues to grow. In these circumstances, external disequilibrium—and a pressing need for international resources—is the only alternative to a slowing-up or definite contraction of the rate of economic activity.[2]

We do not agree with Prebisch. For reasons we shall discuss later, we are not as sanguine as he apparently is about the possibilities of developing sizable exports of manufactured goods on the part of the developing countries. On the contrary, it appears to us that the principal way out of the post-import substitution crisis is to be found for a considerable period in the amplification of the national market for the products of a developing nation's manufacturing enterprises.

Prerequisites for Development in
Post-Import Substitution Phase

From the point of view of the economy as a whole, the basic prerequisite for further development in the post-import substitution phase is a change in those institutions which keep a large percentage of the total population out of the market and which keep certain sectors of the economy lagging considerably behind others. On the one hand, therefore, elements which have hitherto lived in a more or less complete subsistence economy must be incorporated into that part of the economy which provides goods and services for sale and in return constitutes a market for other commodities and services. On the other hand, segments of the economy which, because of existing institutional arrangements, have not been able to provide needed raw materials and foodstuffs, which under other circumstances they might be able to supply, must be reorganized so that they can make a larger contribution to the general national economy.

From the point of view of the individual enterprise, certain basic changes are also required. It is faced with the fact that what has hitherto been largely a seller's market is increasingly being transformed into a buyer's market. Whereas during the import substitution period the individual firm could usually be certain of its ability to sell virtually anything it could produce, since the needs of the market as a whole were being inadequately met, this is no longer the case.

Under these circumstances, if the individual firm is to continue to grow, or even to hold its own, it will have to do one of two things: it must either extend its sales to elements of the population who hitherto have not been in the market at all, or it must take customers away from other similar firms in its fields.[3] In order to do either of these things it must become concerned with problems of costs of production and quality of its product, which were relatively unimportant during the import substitution phase.

The relative position of the consumer will become stronger in this period. No longer faced with an overall shortage of the goods he wants to buy, he will be able to become more selective. He will tend to purchase from those firms whose costs are lower and whose products are more reliable from a quality standpoint.

Whether one looks at the situation from the point of view of the overall economy or of the individual firm, the post-import substitution phase of development calls for fundamental reforms. In many ways, therefore, it is a more difficult phase than that of import substitution. It inevitably has to be a period of conflict of powerful interests within the community. Traditional rural landlords, industrialists, wage workers, and merchants can no longer more or less peacefully follow their own interests without serious clashes with one another. In particular, the needs of the landlord group and those of the urban sectors come into sharp conflict in a way which was not true in the import substitution period. Struggles for power over a wide range of particular issues are inevitable.

Traditional Landholding System

In most developing countries the single most important reform called for in the post-import substitution phase of development is that in land tenure. Most developing countries are characterized by a system under which the accessible arable land has traditionally been in the hands of a very small part of the population who have possessed very large holdings. The great majority of the rural population has lived on the land without owning it, working under a vast variety of sharecropping, tenancy, squatting, or peonage arrangements.

Although the landlord has received his money income from that portion of the output of his holding which has been destined for sale, much of his income has been in kind. He has received provisions for his table, work on construction and maintenance of his mansion and other buildings, and personal service in his rural and even in his urban home as part of his income.

Furthermore, being a large landholder in many of the developing countries has had much more than economic significance. It has provided great social prestige, has assured extensive political influence in the general community, and has given the landowner vast control over the lives and persons of his dependents.

From an economic point of view, the large landholding system tradtional in many, if not most, developing countries has provided relatively little incentive for development. So long as the landlord received the income which he deemed as sufficient to support him at a desired level, he was little concerned with how efficiently or inefficiently his holdings were being worked. Frequently, conspicuous consumption was a part of the process of maintaining one's prestige as a member of the landed elite, and thus there was little incentive to divert income from this consumption to investment in improving the efficiency of his holdings. If the landlord were to divert some income from consumption it was more likely to be for the purpose of buying more land, or at the very least in buying urban real estate, rather than in capitalization of his existing plantations.

From the point of view of the tenants, sharecroppers, or squatters on the large landlord's acres there was also little incentive to invest. In such parts of the plantation as they cultivated for their own account, they were principally engaged in producing for the immediate needs of their families, having only a small surplus for barter or sale at a pittance in the nearest local market. They were all too aware that any improvments they might make on their landlord's holding would redound largely to his benefit rather than theirs. Even small holders living in the vicinity of large plantations were likely to be discouraged from improving their plots too much, for fear of arousing avarice of their large neighbor, who might well use his political influence and economic power to displace them and seize their land.

Minifundia present another series of problems, different from those involved in the latifundia we have just described, although similar in their results. In many of the developing countries a more or less substantial part of the rural population lives on exceedingly small landholdings. Producing little more than enough to provide the barest of livings for their owners, these holdings have the added disadvantage that they actively encourage erosion and the destruction of the soil. Cultivated in the most primitive way, with virtually no capital equipment, and often involving a shifting type of cultivation, these minifundia holdings are as little likely to bring development to agriculture as are those of the latifundia.

Thus, the persistence during the import substitution period of the traditional landholding patterns has the result that that portion of agriculture producing for the national market tends to lag increasingly behind the rest of the economy. It keeps a large part of the population as subsistence farmers, earning little or no money income and being more or less completely out of the market for goods and services produced by other segments of the economy. At the same time it makes agriculture unable to meet the demands of the urban sectors for raw materials and foodstuffs.

In addition, the rural areas become unable even to support their own populations. With the rapid growth in population which has resulted from the dramatic drop in the death rate of most developing countries, a growth which is particularly intense in the rural areas, conditions in the countryside tend to deteriorate during the import substitution period. A growing part of the rural population is "underemployed" or is subject to "hidden unemployment" (defined as a situation in which total output would not be decreased by the removal of these workers).

As a result of this situation, vast numbers of rural people flock to the cities, a movement which is intensified by the changes which industrialization is bringing about in the urban areas. However, industrialization is generally not able to provide steady jobs as quickly as the country folk are migrating, and resources are insufficient to provide these migrants with the housing and public services which they should have. The result is that to some degree hidden unemployment is transferred from the rural to the urban areas, and the cities of the developing countries are increasingly characterized by huge squatter colonies of recent migrants.

Agrarian Reform

Although for reasons which we have discussed earlier, pressure for a change in the traditional rural landholding pattern may not assume major proportions during the import substitution period, since it does not seriously hamper the process of industrialization and general economic development, this is no longer the case once the import substitution phase is passed. When expansion of the market becomes the *sine qua non* of further development, agrarian reform becomes a matter of first priority.

At that point, it becomes of major importance to alter rural institutional arrangements and particularly landholding patterns. General economic development requires that the land be put in the hands of those who will respond more or less quickly to incentives to grow more for the urban market and who in doing so will convert themselves into larger buyers (or buyers for the first time) of goods and services produced by that market.

In most cases, this means that the traditional large landholding system must be abolished and the land be transferred in one way or another to the former tenants, sharecroppers, or squatters. At the same time, the minifundia system must also be attacked through procedures which will consolidate too small holdings into ones large enough to provide an acceptable income to their holders and incentive for measures to improve production and productivity.

It is obvious that agrarian reform is not likely to take place without a subststantial political struggle. In most cases the large landholders will fight strongly to preserve their ownership of the land, which provides them not only with income but with a position of high prestige and substantial power.

However, changes which have come about during the import substitution period will tend to make it possible to overcome the resistence of the landlords. The process of industrialization, together with the growth of the urban area, will have shifted considerably the political balance of power. The wealth of the industrialists is apt to be considerably greater than that of the traditional landlords by the end of the import substitution period, while their influence in the national government is likely to have grown at the expense of that of the landlords. Furthermore, when the facts surrounding the end of the import substitution phase of development begin to dawn fully upon the industrialists, they are likely to see with increasing clarity that it is in their own interests that the rural landholding patterns be changed. Therefore, their influence, which during the import substitution period is likely either to be neutral on the question, or positively hostile to the idea of taking away property from one group and giving it to another, will be more inclined to be exerted in favor of agrarian reform.

Several different kinds of measures may be needed as part of the agrarian reform, in addition to provision for the actual transfer of landholdings. For instance, the extension of the right to vote to illiterates, in countries where literacy has been a requirement for the franchise, may be useful to enfranchise the peasantry. In at least some countries the rural landlords' control over their dependents, as well as their ability to evade the literacy requirement for voting in regard to those dependents who would vote as the landlord told them to, has been one of the principal vehicles through which the landed element has extended its political influence over the nation as a whole.

A second measure which may accompany and complement the agrarian reform is the unionization of rural workers. Unionization is likely to be fought almost as strongly by the traditional rural landlords as is agrarian reform itself. This is because the establishment of effective unions among his workers will not only sharply increase the landowner's labor costs and thus endanger his source of income, but will endanger his position as the unchallenged master of his plantation and the region surrounding it.

Both unionization of rural workers and agrarian reform itself may serve to transform the landlords into modern agricultural entrepreneurs. As the result of increased labor costs resulting from unionization, the landlords may be forced to adopt a new attitude toward their holdings, rationalizing their operations through investment in capital equipment and other imputs designed to increase productivity and reduce costs. If the landlords are allowed by agrarian reform authorities to maintain possession of part of their former holdings, they may find themselves forced to take similar measures in order to continue to enjoy the kind of incomes to which they have become accustomed.

Agrarian reform and measures which accompany it will destroy once and for all the economic and political influence of the traditional landlord class. Although members of this class may be able to maintain some of their social prestige and position because of the respect in which they have tradtionally been held, and because some of their junior members may be sought as marriage partners by newly rich elements of the industrialist and commercial classes, they will have lost the principal bases upon which their previous power and importance was based.

As a result of the decline in the economic and political influence of the traditional rural landlord class, that of the classes which have been the principal proponents of economic development will be increased. Both the middle-class industrialist, commercial, and white-collar elements and the working class groups will experience gains in relation to their ability to influence government policy and programs.[4]

Investment Needs of Agriculture

A change in land tenure arrangements, however, is not the only reform required after the expiration of the import substitution process. If the general process of national economic development is to continue, it is essential that there be heavy investment in the agricultural sector of the economy.

If agriculture is to become more productive, a major requirement is that the agriculturalists be provided with adequate credit, not only for financing their crops but for expanding their capital equipment. Such credit needs will be felt not only by the beneficiaries of the agrarian reform, but by other independent landowners and those traditional landowners who will try to convert the remains of their former holdings into productive business enterprises.

Extensive expenditures will also be required for assuring prices to the agriculturalists which will encourage production. If the farmers are to be stimulated to produce those goods which are most required by the national market, they must be insured by government-guaranteed minimum prices against sudden reduction in the prices of their commodities resulting from temporary increases in supply.

Considerable investments will also be required for developing the infrastructure of agriculture. As in the import substitution phase, the construction of roads will be required, but a different emphasis will be needed in this program. Instead of major concentration on trunk highways binding together the principal centers of population, emphasis will now be required on the building of neighborhood and market roads, linking the arterial highways with agricultural areas which have hitherto had no way of getting their output to market.

Similarly, there will have to be some shift in the emphasis of electric power development during the post-import substitution phase. Considerable concentration will have to be given to extending electrical facilities to the rural areas, for improvement of agricultural and grazing production as well as for helping to raise the living standards of the rural population in order to encourage them to remain in agriculture.

A new direction will also have to be given to education. The provision of at least primary education for rural folk, to make them more able to learn and use the knowledge essential to modern agriculture, will have high priority.

It will also be necessary to develop facilities for training agriculturalists and developing new production techniques. For this purpose, a nationwide system of extension services, including experimental farms and facilities for informing the individual farmers of the latest innovations in seeds, soil conservation, crop rotation, and other methods of improving agricultural techniques, will be required.

Similarly, new emphasis will be necessary in the public health field. The provision of adequate medical and hospital facilities for people of the rural areas will have a high priority which it did not have in the import substitution phase.

Finally, there will be need for investment in what is now generally called "community development." Such programs will serve to mobilize local labor for improvement of the social overhead—schools, water supply, sewerage systems—of rural villages, as well as to develop local industries to carry out the first steps in processing agricultural commodities and even making handicraft goods to serve the rural market.

All these investments will require substantial changes in government policy. They will be expensive, as will the agrarian reform, and will mean that the limited quantity of government funds, the expenditure of which in the import substitution period was largely concentrated in the urban areas to stimulate industry and meet the needs of the burgeoning cities, will have to be diverted in considerable part to the rural sector. Means will also have to be found for channeling increasing quantities of private capital into the rural economy.

Such reforms in government expenditure policy will certainly not be made without resistance. The political influence of the beneficiaries of agrarian reform and other rural elements will have to be brought to bear in favor of such changes. Hopefully, increased agricultural production will result in a decline in the prices of foodstuffs, which constitute 50 to 75 percent of the budget of most working-class families in the developing countries, and such a decline will constitute a strong argument in favor of continued expenditures designed to increase the output and productivity of agriculture. Also, at least some of the resources for these expenditures can be obtained as the result of higher agricultural output and income.

Such a program of structural change and massive investment in agriculture will in some degree represent a different kind of import substitution. In contrast to the situation in what we have called the import substitution phase of development, when all efforts were concentrated on stimulating the growth of enterprises which could produce replacements for manufactured goods formerly obtained from abroad, in this new post-import substitution period emphasis will be on stimulating the output of agricultural products which to an increasing degree have had to be imported.

However, attention should be centered not only on agriculture. Mining industries serving the needs of national industry should also receive emphasis. The search for adequate supplies of coal, iron, nonferrous minerals, and other raw materials for the country's manufacturing enterprises should also be intensified. In most developing countries, no really adequate survey of the nation's mineral wealth will have been undertaken in the export or import substitution phase of development.

Problems of Depressed Areas

Shifts in emphasis among sectors of the economy will need to be accompanied by shifts from the regions in which development tended to be concentrated during the import substitution period. During import substitution, development was centered in those parts of the nation which were already most highly developed, where import substitution would work to greatest advantage. As a result, appreciable parts of the country were left far behind in the development process.

Of course, this problem of depressed areas is not one confined to developing countries. During recent decades such highly industrialized nations as Great Britain and the United States have been faced with the urgent need to do something about those parts of their economies which have lagged behind the general level of development.

In the case of the developing countries, the question of depressed areas is of peculiar importance, because a large part of that segment of the population which is out of the market is concentrated in such regions. It is also in these areas that the possibility of social discontent and possible explosion is most pressing. During the post-import substitution period social struggles are likely to be most critical there since it is there that the traditional and preindustrial society is most firmly entrenched.

At the same time, however, the depressed areas provide some of the greatest possibilities for continuing a high rate of general development. If government and private resources are diverted to them, there may take place within these regions a kind of import substitution process in miniature. With the use of local resources and of personnel and capital from outside, new industries may be fomented there to supply the needs of the people of the vicinity for consumer goods. These industries at the same time may provide more ample markets for capital equipment and more complicated types of consumer goods coming from other parts of the country.

Public policy will have to be altered to concentrate more extensive government investment into these depressed regions. At the same time, it will probably be advisable to offer tax inducements and other advantages to firms which are willing to establish enterprises in these areas.

Other Changes in Government Policy   *Expenditure policy*

Most of the changes in public policy which we have so far noted as being appropriate and urgent in the post-import substitution period have as one of their objectives the incorporation into the national market of large segments of the agricultural population which have remained apart from it during the import substitution phase of development. However, these rural groups are not the only ones who need to be brought more fully into the money economy if economic development is to continue. There are appreciable elements in the urban areas who are little more than on the fringes of the market by the end of import substitution. Changes in government policy, particularly in terms of taxes and expenditures, are required if these elements are also to be made an integral part of the national market.

Most of the marginal elements of the urban population are to be found in the shantytowns, which are such a conspicuous characteristic of most of the cities of the developing countries. Many of the shantytown residents are at best casual laborers or very low-paid domestic servants. In terms of family security, they are constantly on the verge of financial disaster, and they are at best a precarious source of demand for the country's output of consumer goods and services.

The shantytown residents also constitute a grave social and political danger to the rest of the urban society. They are a kind of ever-present time bomb. It is true that the first generation of migrants to these areas experience a considerable thrust of upward social and economic mobility from the status which they knew in the rural areas from which they came. They are not, therefore, prime subjects for social unrest and political revolt as many outside observers of their conditions would judge them likely to be. However, the same cannot be said about the children of these migrants. Having always lived in the shantytowns, on the edges of the more prosperous sections of the cities, their aspirations are higher than those of the original migrants. They have not had the personal experience of having their lot markedly improved by moving from a rural to an urban environment. Hence, if the situation and status of the second generation shantytown residents does not visibly improve, they are apt to become increasingly disaffected from the society around them and tinder for violent civil explosions.

Unemployment and severe underemployment constitutes one of the basic causes of the marginality of the shantytown dwellers. In the post-import substitution phase it is a matter of high priority to supply these people with jobs that will provide them an income which will serve to expand the national market and enable them to contribute toward the solution of the crisis of the cities. Although continued industrialization and the expansion of service trades will be of some use in providing new employment, government will have to bear a considerable part of the burden of supplying new jobs.

At least two kinds of government expenditures will be of primary importance in this regard. The first of these is housing. Not only do the shantytowns themselves need to be converted into permanent residential suburbs, but other large areas of the cities, inhabited by manual workers and even by some white-collar workers, require rebuilding.

A second field of urban expenditure which should have a high priority call on governmental resources during the post-import substitution period is that of providing the cities with adequate public services. By the end of the import substitution phase it is likely to be the case that only a fraction of the urban population will have available to it such facilities as electricity, potable water supplies, and sewerage.

Both the construction industry and the installation of public services call for large quantities of unskilled or partially skilled labor. They, therefore, provide very useful sources of employment for the residents of the shantytowns and should be able to supply jobs for those elements of the population for a generation.

Problem of Inflation

In the post-import substitution period the effect of inflation on economic development is likely to be different from that in the earlier phase. So long as the problem facing the economy is that of accumulating the capital and personnel necessary to turn out the goods demanded by an existing market, considerably increased costs arising from inflation can be pushed forward to the consumer without seriously hampering the process of development itself. However, once the problem becomes one of extending the market, inflation tends to become a drawback to further development. It will become important, therefore, for governments to follow policies which will limit inflation.

Both short-run and long-run policies will be necessary for dealing with inflation. In the short run, it will be advisable for governments to seek more energetically to curb budget deficits, and particularly expenditures which do not contribute to economic development. Perhaps selective credit controls, designed to limit credit to the proportions of the other resources available, and to funnel it into those economic activities which are most conducive to development, will also be useful.

In the longer run, however, the general policies necessary for development in the post-import substitution phase are also likely to help the struggle against inflation. This is particularly the case with regard to government investments in agriculture. Since a majority of the expenditures of most workers in the developing countries is spent on food, a reduction in food prices resulting from the growth of agriculture is apt to have a major impact on the general price level. This reduction in the cost of food will mean a considerable increase in the workers' real wages, a fact which should be useful in limiting pressure for increases in money wages, and hence in labor costs.

Increased concern of the entrepreneurs for the efficiency of their enterprises should also help to diminish inflationary pressures. The whole emphasis of management on reducing costs of production, in order to meet the pressures of competition and the need to expand the market, will, if successful, result in a decrease in the prices of manufactured goods, another major item in determining the general price level.

Even the emphasis of entrepreneurs on trying to improve the quality of their output will make a contribution to a reduction in the price level. It should result in the production of commodities which last longer and have to be replaced less frequently. The real price of these better quality goods will thus be lower than that of the commodities formerly on the market.

Education Needs

Another sector of society which has tended to be comparatively overlooked during the import substitution period but which can no longer be so during the post-import substitution phase of development is education. Although some effort will have been made to provide elementary education to urban children, the schooling of rural youth will have been virtually ignored. Also, only a beginning is likely to have been made during the import substitution period at transforming the quality of education offered by the public school system.

However, the national needs during the post-import substitution era will be different. If emphasis is to be placed in public policy on developing a productive agriculture capable of supplying the needs of the national market, it will be necessary to extend the educational system to the rural areas. Not only will farm children need to be given the rudiments of a general education, but they will also need specific training in agricultural techniques. From them will largely have to be chosen those who go on to get a more advanced education which will permit them to become the experimenters, the agronomists, the agricultural experts that will be required by the new and refurbished agriculture.

At the same time, there will be new educational needs in the urban areas. As industry becomes more conscious of problems of cost of production and of quality, it will need more highly skilled workers, and new emphasis will have to be placed on vocational training. As manufacturing and commercial enterprises become more concerned with rationalizing their operations, there will be an intensified demand for clerical workers and people with other kinds of white-collar and semiprofessional skills. On all levels of the economy and in government there will be need for greater numbers of people with professional, scientific, and technical training and ability.

Thus during the post-import substitution phase of development there will be need not only for a vast augmentation of the number of children and young people in school and facilities for educating them, but for a basic change in the quality of the educational system. The transformation of the school from an institution to train the sons of the elite how to continue to maintain themselves as the elite, into one which gives at least some education to all and is adapted to the training needs of an increasingly complex economy and society, a process which was merely begun during the import substitution period, will now have to receive major emphasis if development is to continue.

This transformation will require new emphasis on the higher levels of education. The secondary schools and the universities will have to expand at an even more rapid pace than the primary educational institutions. Like the lower schools, these higher-level institutions will have to become more diversified in their offerings, with particular emphasis on the technical, scientific, and social science requirements of the new society.

Need for Private Capital Market

Another major reform which is of high priority in the post-import substitution period of development is an alteration of the way in which private firms raise their capital. During the import substitution phase there have been two principal sources of capital funds for most enterprises: ploughing back profits into family-held firms, and borrowing by these firms from the government or from government banks or development corporations. For various reasons, these are inconvenient methods of raising funds during the post-import substitution period.

First, the need to depend to a large degree on ploughed-back profits for expansion has required that such profits be very high. During the import substitution period, high profits could be passed on as high costs of the goods sold by these firms. But when, in the post-import substitution period, high costs of production hamper the process of expanding the market, a process which is essential to further development, this method of financing new investment becomes a positive drawback to the further expansion and growth of the economy.

Second, as we have noted, during the post-import substitution phase there will be increased calls upon the financial resources of the government. It will, therefore, be advisable to restrict governmental expenditures on certain items which were of primary importance during the import substitution period, but which might be met by other sources thereafter. Hence, to the degree possible the government will need to withdraw from the task of financing industry.

The most obvious new source of capital funds which was

largely untapped during the import substitution period is the savings of middle- and modest-income recipients. There is apt to exist a sizable element among professional classes, white-collar workers, and even better-paid manual workers who would be willing under certain conditions to buy shares of stock and who could provide substantial quantities of funds for industrial and commercial enterprises.

However, two factors are likely to have been the principal impediments to the development of such a relatively broad private capital market. In the first place, most firms in industry and commerce will have continued to be held by members of a single family or by a relatively small group of insiders; we shall have more to say about this subsequently. In the second place, most developing countries will not have organized adequate capital markets during the import substitution phase, when there seemed to be no great need for them.

As a result of this situation, those who might have been a sizable source of investment funds for industries during the import substitution period never become accustomed to purchasing stocks or other securities. Their hesitation to do so was intensified by the fact that in many of the developing countries "stock-jobbing" and swindles were all too common in this field.

An institutional change of considerable priority during the post-import substitution period, therefore, will be the organization of securities markets on a firm basis. To this end, legislation will undoubtedly be required which will tend to assure honesty in the dealings in these markets; and perhaps some kind of tax incentives will be needed as an inducement to potential purchasers of securities to put their savings into stocks or bonds of industrial and commercial enterprises.

A second major change in legislation in this same general field will undoubtedly need to be that governing the banking system. Since the banking systems in most developing countries evolved during the period when these nations were expanding their primary product export sector, these systems were designed principally to serve short-term commercial needs. Basically, they came into existence to handle the requirements of the export-import trade. In many, if not most, cases private banks were actually forbidden to make long-term investments of the kind required by manufacturing firms.

In countries in which the private banking system is of the kind we have just described, legislation will have to be changed not only to permit but to encourage at least some private lending institutions to provide capital on a long-term basis. Such private credit can take the place of funds which during the import substitution period came from government banks, which can now turn their attention to more immediately urgent sectors as agricultural development and housing.

· Obviously, these reforms will meet a mixed reception from the industrialist group. Many of them may be slow in seeing the need for an expansion of the private capital market, preferring to keep control of their enterprises in relatively few hands rather than having to resort to issuance of stock to the "general public." They may also be reluctant to exchange reliance for credit upon government institutions with which they are acquainted for dependence upon private banks with which they have little or no experience.

Problem of Foreign Investment

During the post-import substitution period the developing country will face a different situation with regard to foreign investment from that which previously existed. Nationalist arguments against such investment by foreign firms may in some cases be more reasonable than was formerly the case.

During the import substitution stage, foreign investors have two basic factors to contribute to development. First, they can offer capital equipment, and the foreign exchange with which to purchase it, which is required for industrialization. During this period, the machinery and other capital goods required is not available within the developing country and so must be brought in from abroad.

Second, foreign investors can provide know-how which is also essential. Foreign firms bring with them the personnel to put capital goods into operation and to organize the enterprise to use it.

However, after the conclusion of the import substitution process, the urgency for receiving these inputs from abroad may well have been considerably reduced. In the case of a large developing country, with extensive population and resources, the import substitution process may have provided the nation with a well-integrated industrial structure, capable of providing not only most types of consumer goods but a wide variety of capital goods as well. Under these circumstances, the country will be able in further stages of its development to provide virtually all the capital equipment which this development may require. At the same time, the growth of a highly integrated industrial structure will have resulted in the training of a complexity of entrepreneurial and managerial personnel large enough to reduce the marginal need for imported managers.

In the case of a similar developing country, with less population and less ample resources, the import substitution process would not have created such an extensive potential for producing the nation's capital goods needs. Such a country might still have to depend on imports for equipment needed to continue development during the post-import substitution period.

In a developing country with an industrial network adequate to produce most of the capital equipment it needs for further development, there may be a strong case for a very cautious attitude toward an extension of foreign investment. Aside from nationalist arguments against "dependence" upon foreign economies, it may be suggested that new foreign investment which might otherwise be spent on goods and services would, without this investment, not be available to the country's inhabitants. It might also be argued that permitting the importation of capital goods which could be manufactured within the country would have the effect of depriving national producers of a volume of business which would permit them to get the advantages of large-scale production.

Revision of Labor and Social Legislation

Another area of reform required for continuation of rapid development in the post-import substitution period which is within the competence of the government is that of alteration of labor and social legislation. One need is to make the impact of this legislation less costly, and thus to help reduce labor costs. Another is to grant a greater degree of independence from government control to organized labor than it possesses in many developing countries, thus helping to rationalize the process of collective bargaining.

Social security is one of the branches of labor and social legislation which is often most in need of reform. It has frequently developed in bits and pieces, with a great deal of duplication of administration. The consolidation of all branches of social security into a single system is in such a case essential as a means of reducing its costs to both workers and employers.

Legislation which will free the organized labor movement of excessive government control and provide it with its own financial resources adequate to the needs of union administration and collective bargaining is also of considerable importance. With such financial strength, the labor unions will be in a position to pay full-time leaders and to employ economists, engineers, and other technical personnel. Such personnel will make it more feasible for unions to prepare adequate studies of the situation of their respective industries and of the economy as a whole, and thus be able to engage in more realistic bargaining.

Some kinds of protective labor legislation which have developed during the import substitution phase may so add to cost that they act as a drawback to the development during the succeeding period. Such, for instance, may be the case with laws which make it virtually impossible to discharge workers, or make it necessary for employers to keep in reserve large funds with which to pay off workers who are discharged. It may be advisable to repeal or modify such legislation as a means of reducing real labor costs, and thus of stimulating further development.

Changes in Fiscal Policies

One of the major reforms required to assure continued development in the post-import substitution period is a change in fiscal policy. Such a change must affect both the government's expenditures and its sources of income.

As we have indicated, there will be need for new or expanded government expenditures in such fields as agricultural development, housing, and education. We have also indicated that at least some of these increased expenditures can be offset by declines in funds previously alloted to the development of manufacturing. Hopefully, it should also be possible to reduce costs of the military establishment. If this proves impossible, at least attention might be centered on means of using the military more extensively for economic development projects and programs.

It is also to be expected that total government revenues will expand substantially during the post-import substitution period. In part, this will come about as a result of the further development of the economy, which other things being equal will increase the revenues of the state.

Changes in tax policies will also be required in the post-import substitution period. Previously, the governments of most developing countries will have drawn the bulk of their revenues from indirect taxes, levied on a wide variety of goods and services. These taxes serve to increase the market price of the goods on which they are imposed.

Likewise, the tax system existing at the end of the import substitution period is likely to have little relevance to the principle of ability to pay. Those with lowest money incomes tend to be most heavily taxed, while those with larger incomes bear relatively little of the burden of imposts. Rural landlords in particular are apt to be virtually free of taxation.

The post-import substitution phase of development requires drastic alteration of this system of taxation. One method of reducing the market price of goods and services, and thus making them available to a wider range of customers, is to reduce the heavy taxes laid upon those goods and services.

In place of the indirect imposts which should be reduced in order to bring down prices, income taxes and other direct levies will have to be increased in order to provide the government with income which it will need in order to meet its increased responsibilities for economic development and social changes. One hitherto untapped resource which should become available during the post-import substitution period is taxes on landlords with large holdings.

The change in tax policies will require the same shift in political power which will be necessary to make possible other reforms that will be necessary at the end of the import substitution phase to permit further economic development. The urban areas will need virtually as much power in national politics to impose real estate and income taxes on rural landlords as to enact agrarian reform or rural unionization.

Reforms in the Enterprise

Since the major problem facing the individual firm in the post-import substitution period is the expansion of its market, it must, therefore, pay some attention to the cost and quality of its product which it did not have to pay previously. This will make it necessary for the firm to modify its method of operation in various respects if it is to continue to expand, or even to maintain, its own share of the market. It must seek to reduce various kinds of costs, and it must seek to improve the quality of the goods or services which it produces.

The costs of virtually all the imputs used by industrial and commercial firms need consideration if overall costs of production are to be reduced. These include the costs of raising capital, of management, and of labor. Reforms are undoubtedly called for in all these fields, as we have noted.

We have already seen the need for the development of a private capital market, in the form of securities exchanges and private investment banks. However, from the point of view of the individual firm, a further change in traditional policy is needed. During the import substitution period the typical industrial firm was likely to be one controlled by a single family, or at most by a small number of insiders. If firms are to reduce their costs of raising capital for further expansion, they will have to move away from the family firm pattern.

The economics of competition may force family groups to forego 100 percent control of their enterprises. A reduction in the profits, which have hitherto been necessary to provide capital for expansion, and have been passed on as added costs to the consumer, becomes necessary if the enterprise is to be able to compete effectively or to extend its clientele to elements of the population which have hitherto been outside of the market. Profits can thus no longer be the only or principal source of new capital. The firm will have to raise new funds from a large number of small and medium-sized investors.

This change will be very difficult for many entrepreneurs. They will be loath to allow "outsiders" to have any participation in the ownership of their enterprises. However, the pressure of competition will make them increasingly aware of the need for such an alteration of policy. In any case, as experience in already industrialized countries shows, relinquishment of 100 percent control will not necessarily mean, for some time at least, that dominant families will be unable to have a contolling interest in the firms they established.

Somewhat the same problem will be faced by owners of industrial firms insofar as their management personnel is concerned. If management of these enterprises is to be efficient enough to compete adequately with its rivals and to produce goods of lower cost and better quality, it will have to become more professional. In part, this means that the decision as to who should have managerial positions can no longer be based only or even primarily on family relationship with principal stockholders in the enterprise, but rather on their efficiency as managers. It will mean that there must be compartmentalization and specialization in managerial functions.

One effect of this change will be that the dominant families in industrial enterprises will have to draw more and more on the talents of those who do not belong to the family or the small "insider" group. Furthermore, they will have to give growing responsibility and authority to such outsiders, who are likely to become increasingly resistant to working exclusively for the benefit of the dominant ownership group.

In addition, it will become increasingly apparent to the dominant elements in the industrial enterprises that their executives need special training. Hence, the demand for formal facilities for training executives, whether through schools of business in recognized universities or special training programs sponsored by the enterprises themselves, is apt to grow rapidly.

The need for specialization of function in management will become apparent in the post-import substitution phase of development. People particularly prepared to deal with problems of production, marketing, and personnel management will be increasingly in demand if industrial firms are to adequately organize to meet the demands of competition and of seeking out new customers among those who have hitherto not purchased the goods the manufacturing firms produce.

One additional function of management, which has generally not been assumed in the import substitution period, will have to be undertaken during the subsequent phase of development. This is the area of "research and development."

In the import substitution phase it will usually have been the case that national industries in the developing country will have depended largely, if not wholly, on the research and development facilities of companies in the already industrialized countries. Many of the pioneer firms will in any case be branches of corporations based in the industrially more advanced nations and will have available to them the results of work of their parent firms' laboratories. Moreover, even nationally owned enterprises will have depended largely on patent licensing and other agreements with foreign firms for the technology and processes which they have used, and for changes in these.

However, this is likely to become increasingly inconvenient in the post-import substitution period. If the goods turned out by national industries are to be adapted more closely to local demand, so as to have a wider market, the industrial firms operating in the country will have to depend more on their own ability to innovate, to create new products, and to adapt existing ones to local needs.

Furthermore, there will be advantages in finding ways to use hitherto untapped raw material resources within the national boundaries, materials which, once their use has been discovered, may well be considerably cheaper than former standard goods brought in from outside or produced at a relatively higher cost within the country. It cannot be expected that firms based in the already industrialized countries will give high priority to reasearch and development involving this kind of potential raw materials in the developing nations. The burden of such activity will lay with the governments and firms of the developing countries.

The development of national research and development facilities may also be very useful in solving another problem faced by most of the developing nations, that of the so-called brain drain. Relatively well-trained physical and social scientists in the developing nations tend to find a very limited field of employment in their native countries, which is one of the main reasons causing them to migrate abroad, particularly to the more highly industrialized nations. A growing apparatus of research and development at home can provide many of these people with ways of using their talents and training and making a comfortable living at home.

There will also, of course, be a nationalist argument in favor of such research and development activity in the developing countries. As those nations become less dependent upon other nations for supplying the basic consumer needs, and many of the capital requirements, of their economies, there will still remain considerable concern about the "technological dependence" of these countries on the more industrialized powers. Inevitably science and technology have a large international component, but a country completely devoid of research and development facilities of its own is in danger of being cut off from an essential component for the future development of its economy and society.

Other changes which will be taking place during the post-import substitution period should aid those firms that will be establishing a research and development operation. This is particularly the case with the growth of a more complex education system, which is capable of turning out a great variety of scientists and technicians, some of whom can be incorporated into research and development departments.

Some of the burden for research and development will undoubtedly have to be borne by the government. This is likely to be the case with regard to agriculture, the search for natural resources, and the carrying on of basic scientific research. Also, it will undoubtedly be necessary for the government, through tax and other policies, to encourage the activities of private firms in the areas of research and development.

Another dimension of the post-import substitution crisis is indicated by the need to shift from "development in breadth" to "development in depth." The Economic Commission for Latin America study, *Problemas y perspectivas del desarrollo industrial latinoamericano,* has indicated the situation which faces industrial entrepreneurs when it is no longer feasible for them to reinvest their profits in expansion into some new area of import substitution. This study says:

> However, widespread development in breadth tends to increase and perpetuate a situation of monopoly or restricted competition and cause the stagnation of traditional industries. This is apparently one reason why such industries in Latin America are now faced with an urgent need to renew the obsolete equipment they have accumulated, and why their levels of organizational and operational efficiency are so low.[5]

Thus, when development in breadth is no longer possible because of the exhaustion of import substitution opportunities, the entrepreneurs are forced to come to grips with the problems of high costs, inefficient operations, and poor quality. They must invest more intensively in the enterprises which they already have, instead of moving into an entirely new area of import substitution, and must rationalize and make more efficient their firms' operations.

Finally, firms in the developing countries will have to become more concerned in the post-import substitution phase than they previously were with problems of marketing. Advertising and the study of consumer demand will assume an importance they did not formerly have, when a firm could expect to sell virtually anything it could produce. Of course, the development of the marketing aspect of business administration will be closely connected with its research and development activities.

Conclusion

When a nation moves into the post-import substitution phase of its development, it will face the necessity for a great variety of changes and reforms in its institutions and in its customary patterns of behavior. Some of these will require fundamental changes in public policy, others will involve alterations of the traditional behavior of private institutions, particularly manufacturing and merchandising firms.

The need for reform will be so widespread that countries entering the post-import substitution phase will be faced with a major social, economic, and political crisis. Traditional vested interest, such as those of the rural landlords, which were virtually untouched during the import substitution period, will come under attack. Other vested interests which have developed during the import substitution period itself, such as those of families dominating large manufacturing enterprises, will also be undermined. Even such groups as trade unions may have to undergo basic changes in their methods of operation.

Thus the post-import substitution period presents kinds of problems which did not characterize the era in which economic development could go forward principally through establishing industries to produce goods formerly imported. Import substitution development can take place largely without hurting the interests of any entrenched groups in the economy and society. The traditional landed elite may have to pay somewhat more for its consumer goods, but otherwise its interests are not damaged. Similarly, the commercial and political elites inherited from previous periods are not fundamentally hurt during the import substitution period.

In contrast, during the post-import substitution period,

further economic development is not likely go to forward without hurting, in one way or another, powerful interests in the economy, society, and politics. Thus the completion of the import substitution phase of development is apt to present a country with a serious crisis.

The crisis generated by the end of the import substitution period of development will not be easily or quickly overcome. Indeed, not every country faced with this situation will necessarily undertake the reforms needed for the continuation of economic development. Entrenched economic and social groups may prove strong enough to resist the changes in their power and privileges which are needed for continued progress of the economy. The national consensus may be that the costs of further economic development are too high to be paid.

However, it is unlikely that the ability of entrenched interest groups to resist change will reduce the "revolution of rising expectations." Pressure from lower-class groups to improve their lot—which can be achieved if the general economy continues to grow but may be unattainable if this does not occur—will continue. If further economic development proves impossible, social and political explosion will be virtually inevitable.

NOTES

1. Harry Johnson, "Tariff and Economic Development: Some Theoretical Issues" in *Journal of Development Studies* 1 (October 1964). Reprinted in James D. Theberge, *Economics of Trade and Development* (New York: John Wiley & Sons, 1968), p. 373.

2. Raul Prebisch, *Towards a Dynamic Development Policy for Latin America* (New York: United Nations, 1963), p. 70.

3. Of course, the degree to which a particular firm will be faced with competitors will depend on what has occurred during the import substitution phase. If during that period government policy has too strongly

favored the growth of monopoly, or the smallness of the available market had discouraged the entry of more than one firm in a particular industry, the individual enterprise will not face competition in the import substitution period. However, in most developing countries, except for the very smallest, or those in which in pursuance of some illusory "socialist" dogma the government has actively sponsored monopoly (public or private), there are likely to be two or more firms in most lines of consumer goods production.

4. For a more extensive discussion of agrarian reform in its economic, social, and political aspects, see the author's *Agrarian Reform in Latin America* (New York: Macmillan, 1974).

5. Cited in ECLA, *The Process of Industrial Development in Latin America* (New York: United Nations, 1966), p. 36.

CHAPTER SIX

New Export Possibilities in the
Post-Import Substitution Period

In theory at least, expansion of the internal market is not the only alternative facing a country which has completed the import substitution phase of development. It also should be possible for such a nation to develop new markets abroad for the products of its manufacturing industries.

The First United Nations Conference on Trade and Development underscored the need for developing exports of manufactured goods in the post-import substitution period. One of its resolutions noted: "The development of the new industries is required not only to improve the external balance; since the process of import substitution is, in many countries, about to reach an economic impasse, while in other countries such a situation is bound to arise in the not too distant future, the development of export industries is also a precondition for the continuation of the industrialization process itself."[1]

However, such a process of fomenting overseas markets is not easy. Special difficulties are likely to be encountered in trying to sell the manufactured goods of the developing nations in the already industrialized countries, and even the development of markets in other developing states is not facile.

Special Concessions by Industrialized Countries

Raul Prebisch, in his capacity as Secretary General of the Economic Commission for Latin America, did much to popularize the idea of import substitution. In the early 1960s, he also developed an idea of how to meet the post-import substitution crisis. Convinced that many of the developing countries had gone as far as they could along the road of import substitution, he urged that in order to encourage further development the already industrialized nations should create special conditions favorable to the importation of manufactured goods from the developing countries.

Prebisch supported his argument for this policy on the traditional grounds of the international division of labor. Noting that the highly industrialized countries were accustomed to purchasing many of their raw materials and foodstuffs from the developing ones, he suggested that they should extend this custom to include the purchase of various kinds of manufactured consumer goods, and even in some cases specialized types of capital goods. He argued that if the developing countries were able to produce more efficiently than the highly industrialized ones such commodities as textiles, clothing, shoes, and some kinds of specialized steels, both the developed and underdeveloped countries would be better off if these were produced in the less industrialized countries, and exchanged by them for more complicated kinds of products.

Prebisch professed to see certain trends in the highly industrialized countries which in the early 1960s were favoring the tendency of these nations to purchase at least some of their manufactured goods from the developing areas. In one of his last publications as Secretary General of ECLA, *Towards a Dynamic Development Policy for Latin America,* he wrote:

> In those centres, factors conducive to a more liberal import policy are developing. There is a clear trend towards a pro-

gressive shortage of manpower, particularly in countries where the rate of economic development has been high. This might lead naturally to an acceleration of the growth of the capital-intensive industries that require a relatively small labor input and expand more slowly than the industries which need a relatively large labor force and are less capital-intensive.

If this should be the case, the major centres would have to import the products of the latter in order to meet part of their growing demand. The developing countries would thus find a promising export field for a type of industry which they should be particularly anxious to develop as being highly manpower-absorbing.[2]

He thought, furthermore, that the possibility for such exports from the developing to the developed countries (the periphery to the center, in his terms) would be apt to go considerably beyond products of industries with comparatively simple technology. He wrote:

This does not mean that exports of manufactured goods by the developing countries will have to be confined to the products of industries requiring simple techniques, since there are some with advanced techniques in which the high manpower coefficient might encourage peripheral exports. There may also be industries where the ability of the developing countries to compete depends less on the proportion of better natural resources or other favorable factors, such as differences in the transport costs of exports of raw materials and of manufactured goods.[3]

There are several difficulties, both economic and political, with Prebisch's suggestion. For one thing, it is by no means clear how many of the developing countries could take extensive advantage of such an opportunity to sell manufactured products to the industrialized nations, even if the opportunity were afforded them to do so. Not by any means do all of the developing nations possess textile or shoemaking industries, for instance, which are efficient enough to be capable of producing goods that would undersell the domestic output of the highly industrialized nations. In addition, the industries of the developing countries would be faced with extensive problems of acquainting consumers in the developed nations with their products, with strange trademarks and of quality unknown by their prospective customers.

However, even if these economic difficulties could be overcome, it is likely that the political difficulties facing Prebisch's program are even more formidable. In most of the highly industrialized countries, those industries which Prebisch would like to see enter into competition with their counterparts in the developing nations are "sick," and far from agreeing to a reduction in such protection from foreign competition as they are now benefiting from, they are clamoring for higher tariffs, subsidies, and other help from the governments of their respective nations. Their political influence is appreciable regardless of whatever economic and financial difficulties they may be encountering, and it does not seem likely that the governments of the highly industrialized countries will want to pay the political price which will be exacted in reprisal for granting concessions to their foreign competitors.

Trade With Industrial Countries Without Concessions

Although it seems unlikely that the already industrialized nations will freely open their doors to manufactured goods from the developing countries, this does not by any means indicate that there are no possibilities for the developing countries to sell the products of their factories in the highly industrialized nations. Experience has shown that various kinds of processed foodstuffs, specialized steel products, and some of the output of petrochemical industries in the developing countries can find markets in the more highly developed nations.

Some of the highly industrialized countries may provide

larger markets than others. The rapidly expanding economy of Japan has in recent years shown itself particularly receptive to semiprocessed and even fully manufactured goods from the developing nations, and it seems likely that these possibilities will continue to expand. The Soviet Union and other European Communist countries, as the pressure within them to provide their people with greater quantities of consumer goods grows, may be increasingly willing to obtain at least some of these goods from the developing nations.

As has been the case among the already highly industrialized countries, there may well develop a two-way exchange of similar products between the more advanced developing nations and the highly industrialized ones. Automobiles, motion pictures, and some kinds of machinery might be included in a list of such products which both kinds of nations would purchase from one another.

However, it is not likely that such exports to the economically advanced nations will by themselves take the place of import substitution as the chief motor force for further development. For some time after the end of the import substitution period, the range of manufactured goods likely to be competitive in the highly industrialized countries is apt to remain marginal.

Exports to Other Developing Countries

In the near future, the possibilities for expanding exports of manufactured goods by trade among developing countries seem considerably better than selling the same products to the highly industrialized nations. Several factors tend to favor this.

First of all, economic development is uneven among the developing countries. Some of these countries have advanced far enough to be producers of capital goods. They turn out machinery needed by other developing countries to establish their industries.

Second, as in the rest of the world, natural resources are unevenly distributed among the developing nations. As these countries industrialize, many of them will find that they do not possess all of the raw materials which their new manufacturing enterprises need. As their populations increase, they will have a growing demand for foodstuffs which either cannot be produced at all, or cannot be produced economically within their frontiers, and many of these raw materials and foodstuffs will be available in other developing countries.

Third, in many instances there may be savings possible in transportation costs in trade among the developing countries as opposed to trade between them and the highly industrialized ones. At the present time virtually all the highly developed nations are in the Northern Hemisphere, whereas most of the developing ones are in the Southern. Once transportation facilities are established between developing countries in relatively close proximity to one another, it may well be cheaper to ship sizable quantities of goods across these nearby borders than to import them from long distances.

Finally, one factor which may foster the development of greater trade among the developing countries is the fact that most of these nations face a more or less acute shortage of "hard" foreign exchange. Raul Prebisch has pointed out that the underdeveloped countries generally have a virtually inexhaustible potential demand for the goods and services produced by the industrialized nations. The amount which they purchase is limited only by the amount they can earn by selling their own products—basically raw materials and foodstuffs—to the industrialized powers.

Faced with this situation, the developing countries will frequently be anxious to obtain manufactured goods, including some kinds of consumer products and capital equipment, from other developing nations. However, they will do so only if they can receive goods of competitive price and quality to those which they previously obtained from the great manufacturing nations. The advantage of such purchases will be that they will not have to be paid for in the currencies of the highly industrialized countries, if two-way or multilateral trade can be developed among the developing nations.

In the growth of this commerce among the underdeveloped nations, the latter will not always follow all the niceties of international trading customs and rules. Upon occasion, it may be convenient for two such nations to enter into bilateral arrangements which in some cases may virtually be the equivalent of barter agreements. In other instances, some kind of a bilateral clearing system may be resorted to.

The highly industrialized states would be ill-advised to try to thwart the growth of greater trade, even under somewhat unorthodox conditions, among the developing countries. Although the decision of an underdeveloped nation to purchase some manufactured goods from another developing country will mean that those particular commodities will not be purchased from a highly industrialized nation, this seems hardly likely to decrease the total volume of trade between the underdeveloped and developed countries. The developing countries (with the possible exception of some oil-producing nations) are unlikely to hoard for long the dollars, francs, marks, or pounds sterling which they earn through selling their own products. The total volume of trade between underdeveloped and industrialized nations seems destined for several generations to be determined basically by the amount of products which the latter are willing to purchase from the former.

Common Market Possibilities

A suggestion for fostering trade among the developing countries which is a very popular subject of discussion, resolutions, and conferences in and among those nations is the possibility of establishing common markets or customs unions. Belief in the efficacy of customs unions virtually has the status of revealed truth among the underdeveloped nations. However, so far the record of accomplishment of such common markets is a sparse one.

A common market or customs union is an arrangement between two or more sovereign nations by which they abolish all governmental barriers to trade between themselves, while at the same time raising a common system of barriers to freedom of trade with third parties. It presumably makes possible the benefits of international division of labor among the nations participating in it, and will contribute to the development of all the countries concerned. However, there are various difficulties which have faced the actual achievement of common markets among the developing nations.

These difficulties are both political and economic. On the political level is the reluctance of the developing countries to surrender any part of their sovereignty to an international organization. This attitude is most acute among nations which have recently obtained their independence.

Furthermore, rivalries and enmities among the underdeveloped countries are much greater than observers in the highly industrialized nations sometimes realize. Border disputes, traditional quarrels, and other factors create difficulties for the cooperation necessary for the establishment of a successful common market. Unless it is felt that there are compelling economic reasons for forming an economic union, it will be difficult to overcome these political impediments.

Economic difficulties are perhaps even more formidable. One of the principal economic issues which arises almost immediately in any serious discussions concerning the establishment of customs unions is the unequal stages of development among the nations proposing to join in such a common market. Some of these countries already have extensive consumer goods manufacturing sectors or even capital goods industries, whereas others are merely at the beginning of the industrialization process.

There is fear in the less developed of these nations that if they permit completely free entry of goods from their customs union partners, their own "infant industries" will perish or be seriously damaged in the face of such competition. In such a case, the less developed among the proposed partners will undoubtedly demand some kind of "special treatment" which will permit them to maintain extensive barriers to imports from the rest of the customs union, for fear of becoming mere "economic colonies" of their associate nations. However, the more industrialized partners will be loath to grant any extensive concessions of this kind.

Even in the more advanced countries proposing to join a common market there may well be strong opposition to a customs union on the part of industries which feel their interests might be hurt by competition from their counterparts in the partner nations. In other cases, industrialists concerned principally with expanding the internal market for their products within their own country may see little to be gained by seeking to gain customers in other countries, under unknown conditions, at the risk that firms in those other nations might meanwhile poach on their own markets at home.

An additional economic problem with attempts to form common markets is the lack of experience of the developing countries in trading with one another. The traditional trading pattern of virtually every such nation has been with one or more of the highly industrialized countries, and importers in the developing nation have well established relations with firms in their country's principal trading partners. There will probably be reluctance on the part of importers to substitute unknown enterprises in other developing nations for firms with which they have extensive experience. There may also be fear that diversion of orders from the highly industrialized nations may imperil their country's ability to sell traditional exports to those same highly developed nations.

Alternatives to Customs Unions

Customs unions, therefore, do not seem to be any kind of panacea for the need of these developing countries which have exhausted import substitution possibilities to expand their exports. However, this does not by any means indicate that there is no possibility for the intensification of trade among the developing nations.

Certainly, for the reasons which we have previously noted—uneven development and natural resources, shortages of hard foreign exchange, and possible savings in transportation costs—there will be numerous incentives for the developing nations to intensify trade among themselves. However, such intensification is likely to come about through the enterprise of businessmen of the more industrialized of these states and through trade agreements covering specific products, rather than through general accords to abolish all official impediments to trade.

Foreign Trade Expansion
Vs. Amplifying National Markets

There may well be cases in which national political leaders will seek the development of exports of their country's manufactured goods as an alternative to the apparently more difficult task of expanding their nation's internal market. However, it is not likely that one way of expanding the market for national industries is apt to prove a substitute for the other. Both methods require many of the same reforms in a country which has exhausted the possibilities of import substitution industrialization.

The manufacturing firms of the developing country will have to compete in international trade with those of the highly industrialized nations. They will not benefit, as they did in their homelands during the import substitution period, from a protected market. They can compete effectively overseas with the firms of highly industrialized powers only if their products are cheaper and of at least equal quality.

Thus the industrial firms of the developing countries will have to become equally cost-conscious and quality-conscious, whether they intend to expand their markets within their nation's borders or through exports. They will have to increase the productivity of their labor force: they will have to improve the efficiency of their management. Likewise, they will have to institute closer control over the quality of their products.

It is even doubtful that the cultivation of new markets for industrial products abroad will serve to avoid the kind of reforms in the general society that will be required in order to expand the internal market. The changes in agriculture—agrarian reform, intensified capital investment, and technical assistance—which are needed to provide cheaper substitutes for expensive imported raw materials will be equally required, whether emphasis is to be put on expanding sales of national industries within the country or outside of it.

Thus development of industrial exports and expansion of the internal market are not alternative policies for the post-import substitution period, but rather are complementary. An expansion of the internal market, which will help to provide national industries with the economics of large-scale production, will also help to make these industries competitive in world markets. By driving down costs of production, the effort to expand sales at home will make more feasible sales of the same products abroad.

NOTES

1. *Proceedings of the United Nations Conference on Trade and Development,* Volume IV: *Trade in Manufactures* (New York: United Nations, 1964), pp. 43–44.

2. Raul Prebisch, *Towards a Dynamic Development Policy for Latin America* (New York: United Nations, 1963), p. 72.

3. *Ibid.,* p. 73.

CHAPTER SEVEN

Some Latin American Examples

We have noted earlier that most of the presently developing countries of the world are using the import substitution strategy of development. As a group, the Latin American nations have gone farther along this road than have those of Asia and Africa. Hence, some short summaries of how the Latin American countries have used this strategy may help to illustrate the nature of the strategy as well as its limitations.

In the pages that follow, therefore, we shall look in a cursory fasion at the experience of several Latin American countries with the import substitution strategy. We shall preface these sketches with a brief look at how other Latin American countries have used the alternative strategies sketched at the beginning of this book.

Puerto Rico and the British Strategy

The Latin American area presents only one clear example of a country which has developed in accordance with what we have called the "British strategy of development": through the export of manufactured goods which the country produces as a result of its development efforts. This is the case of Puerto Rico.

It was possible for Puerto Rico to use this strategy only

because it had a peculiar relationship with the United States, with its market of over 200,000,000 people. As a territory of, and subsequently a commonwealth in association with, the United States, it was within the United States tariff walls, and its residents shared citizenship and the currency system with the residents of the mainland. At the same time, Puerto Ricans did not have to pay the United States federal income tax and were able to use tax incentives to attract industry, while sharing in the payments of a wide range of United States federal expenditure programs. Finally, federal tariffs collected in Puerto Rico stayed there, while federal excise taxes collected on the continent on Puerto Rican rum returned to the island.

Puerto Rico's relationship with the United States gave it various advantages from the point of view of using the British strategy of development. In the first place, it provided the island with free access to the mainland market and meant that its industrialization did not have to depend on its own 2.5 million person market, but could be based on the nearly hundred times larger market of the world's richest country.

In the second place, the association with the United States meant that Puerto Rico had direct access to the United States capital market for the extensive bond offerings which its government has made during the process of development for financing expansion of the economic infrastructure of the island. At the same time, Puerto Rico had the advantage that its new industries could attract continental firms on a large scale, and these firms could assure both first-rate efficient management from the beginning, and a market large enough to permit the construction of plants of optimum size. Finally, these U.S.-based firms had well-established channels of distribution in their continental markets and generally were producing goods with brand names well known in the United States. Hence, Puerto Rican manufactured products could be competitive with those of the mainland from the outset.

Of course, Puerto Rico would not have been able to take advantage of the benefits of its close association with the United States if its government had not adopted energetic measures to exploit them. It established an Industrial Development Corporation to build model factories to be sold or leased to new manufacturing firms; a Water Resources Authority to develop a plentiful supply of cheap electricity; a Government Development Bank to help finance some of the new enterprises as well as to act as the government's fiscal agent; and an Economic Development Administration to promote the establishment of new firms in the island and coordinate the whole industrialization effort. The government also carried on extensive programs for improving health conditions, and for vastly expanding the island's educational system.

As a result of this development effort, Puerto Rico received a net increase of 1,200 factories in the first twenty years of the program, the great majority of which sold most of their output on the mainland. The per capita income of the island's inhabitants more than doubled in the same period. Manufactured goods surpassed sugar, the traditional export, as source of income from abroad by the end of the first decade of the use of the British strategies.

Although the Puerto Rican use of the British strategy of development has permitted a very rapid increase in per capita income and the material well-being of the island's inhabitants, it has had some important adverse effects. It has resulted in a very large sector of the Puerto Rican economy being owned by firms located on the mainland, which took their decisions concerning their Puerto Rican operations in the light of what was good for the overall operation of the firms in the United States rather than in the light of what was good for the Puerto Rican economy. Some have argued, too, that excessive concentration on attracting firms that could sell their products in the continental United States has resulted in opportunities for the establishment of enterprises to

meet the needs of the Puerto Rican market having sometimes been overlooked. Finally, the close tie with the United
States market has made Puerto Rico perhaps more susceptible to the business cycle on the continent than it might
otherwise have been.

Soviet and Castro Strategies in Cuba

Castro's Cuba has been the site where both what we have
called the "Soviet" (or forced capitalization) and the "Castro" (or primary product export) strategies of development
have been experimented with. In neither case has the exper-
iment been outstandingly successful.

When Fidel Castro definitely made up his mind to take the
island on a Marxist-Leninist path, Ernesto (Che) Guevara
was placed in charge of the country's economic policy.
Guevara was a firm believer in the Soviet strategy of development. He presided over the establishment of an extensive planning agency, the Junta Central de Planificación,
and was in direct charge of the country's confiscated industries.

In true conformity with the Soviet strategy of development the Castro regime established collective agriculture
and undertook a program of construction of heavy industry.
Castro and Guevara both promised that by 1965 Cuba would
be the proud possessor of the largest steel plant in Latin
America, and other major capital investments were planned
as well.

During this phase, the Castro regime waged unrelenting
war its traditional export industry, sugar. Large areas of
cane were ploughed under, and the place of sugar was taken
by a variety of other crops. At the same time, Castro, Guevara, and other leaders of the regime denounced the "slav-
ery" which sugar had allegedly imposed on the island.

This strategy had disastrous results insofar as the island's economic development was concerned. It resulted in the reduction of sugar production by nearly 50 percent, crop diversification failed, and little progress was made in the development of manufacturing. On the contrary, many of the nation's existing industries were forced to close down because of their inability to obtain spare parts for plants originally built with United States machinery.

Because of the poor showing of the economy as a result of the Soviet strategy of development, Fidel Castro was persuaded to shift to what we have called the "Castro strategy": dependence upon expansion of production of the traditional export in order to obtain the resources necessary for industrialization. This change was made about the end of 1963.

Fidel Castro himself has expressed this strategy of achieving industrialization, in a speech he made at the Cuban Sugar Technological Institute on November 13, 1964. He commented:

> Sometimes our enemies have claimed that we have renounced industrialization. No! In the first place that agricultural development requires the development of industry, and furthermore, in our conditions agriculture is the basis of our development, and agriculture is what will provide the country with the resources necessary for the development of industry in general, because if it were not for sugar, if it were not for the foreign exchange which we obtain from sugar, no ship would enter Cuba, practically no train would move, not a single airplane, a single transport vehicle; without sugar we would not even have light, we would not have the resources which we must import.

In the years during which the Cuban regime applied the Castro strategy of development, it used the most extensive measures to mobilize the population for the basic objective of cutting cane and getting it to the mills. Thus, early in 1968 virtually all small commercial and service enterprises were abolished, and their former owners were sent to the sugar fields. During the final year of the drive for 10 million tons of sugar, virtually every adult and adolescent in the country was mobilized for a longer or shorter period of cane cutting.

In the end, the target of 10 million tons was not achieved, the country falling 1.5 million tons short. Furthermore, even this 8.5 million tons (about 1.5 million more than Cuba had ever produced before) was harvested at the cost of very extensive damage to the rest of the economy. In a July 26, 1970, speech Fidel Castro recounted at length the shortfalls in output in virtually every other sector of the economy, largely as the result of the mobilization of labor and transport facilities for the climactic cane harvest.

After 1970, the Cuban regime reverted to the Stalinist strategy of development. Emphasis was once again put on direct industrialization efforts; the planning mechanism was rationalized. Direct Soviet influence over, if not control of, the process was instituted by the establishment in 1971 of a Joint Soviet-Cuban Technical Commission to supervise the economy, and with the setting up in 1973 of twenty-nine sectoral committees of the same kind.

Latin American Use of Import Substitution

Most of the Latin American countries, however, have used the import substitution strategy of economic development. Their experiences indicate the strengths and limitations of this method of bringing about the development of the economies of underdeveloped nations.

Chile and Brazil provide examples of how the impetus of import substitution can be exhausted, and of the measures which are necessary for a country to enter into the post-import substitution phase. Mexico and Venezuela provide cases in which the kind of problems faced by the other two nations have been at least partially overcome.

The Chilean Post-Import Substitution Crisis

Starting after the War of the Pacific in 1879, in which the Chileans seized the nitrate "pampas" from Bolivia and Peru, the country developed its first major export product, natural nitrates. The export boom based on this product continued until World War One, during which the Germans applied the process which they had developed for taking nitrogen out of the air, thus bringing disaster to the Chilean natural nitrate industry. More than a decade passed until the mining of copper took the place of nitrates as the country's principal export activity. During the nitrate boom, the country developed substantial imports, thus establishing one precondition for import substitution industrialization.

Although some beginnings of industrialization had occurred during the nitrate export boom, it was the Great Depression which gave major impetus to the process of import substitution industrialization. As a result of the drastic decline in the sales of the country's exports during the Depression, Chile was deprived of most of its foreign exchange, a fact which gave automatic protection to Chilean entrepreneurs who established manufacturing firms. Starting in the 1930s also, the government began to use exchange controls, which had originally been thought of merely as a way to ration the drastically limited quantity of foreign currency, as a deliberate means of stimulating industrialization. There was also a substantial increase in tariffs. Finally, in 1939, the Chilean Development Corporation was established by the government for the purpose of financing new industrial enterprises.

Government policy during the 1930s and 1940s stimulated the establishment of import-substituting industries. These included textiles, shoes, light metallurgical goods, pharmaceuticals, and wood products. The government itself established a steel plant and an oil refinery and undertook important infrastructure developments in the fields of electric power and transportation.

During this period, Chilean events followed the import substitution strategy in yet another way. Relatively few efforts were made to stimulate the expansion and modernization of agriculture, and none at all was made to carry out an agrarian reform. As a result, the country was converted between the 1930s and the 1960s from a modest net exporter of agricultural products to a substantial net importer.

By the early 1950s Chile had reached the end of the possibility for import substitution as the main impetus to carry development forward. If economic development was to continue, Chile was going to have to undertake certain reforms which would enlarge the national market.

However, the economic and political leaders were slow to respond to this crisis arising from the end of the import substitution process. Although during the 1950s industrialists did begin to become concerned about improving the quality of their managerial personnel, and various management training courses were established on a permanent basis—with the help of the United States foreign aid program—and the government did establish a technical university to increase the output of skilled workers and foremen as well as of people with more highly developed skills, little was done to bring into the market sizable elements of the population who remained on its fringes or more or less totally outside.

It was not until the election of President Eduardo Frei in 1964 that the Chilean government finally began to undertake the measures needed to deal with the economic stagnation that had characterized the country for nearly a decade and a half. The government immediately authorized the unionization of the workers employed in the country's agriculture and also began a process of agrarian reform. This latter program involved not only the expropriation of large estates—particularly those which were being inefficiently used—but also extensive capital investment in agriculture by the Agrarian Reform Corporation and other government agencies concerned with the reform. These measures were designed, at least in part, to bring the million or more Chileans employed in agriculture more fully into the market, as well as to increase the productivity of the rural sector of the economy, for the purpose of making Chile more self-sufficient in foodstuffs and some agricultural raw materials.

At the same time, the Frei administration sought to expand the economy through augmenting the country's exports. Special attention was given to increasing output of the traditional export, copper, for which the demand and price conditions at that time were favorable. However, in addition, the government undertook to encourage the establishment of a number of new industries, based largely on local raw materials, which could compete in the international market. These included pulp and paper, petrochemicals, fish and seafood and their derivatives, and certain kinds of metallugical products.

The Frei government also sought to widen the scope of possible import substitution on a multinational basis. Chile has a population of only ten million people, which inevitably limits the possibilities of national economic development even based on full participation of the population in the market. The Frei government, as a result, was a strong advocate of the economic unification of Latin America. It took a leading role in bringing into existence the Andean Group, which aspires to form a common market among Venezuela, Colombia, Ecuador, Peru, Bolivia, and Chile by the mid 1980s.

Although the coming to power of the government of President Salvador Allende, dedicated to taking the country down the "Chilean Road to Socialism," in 1970, provoked an extensive degree of economic chaos and finally led to a military coup in September 1973, it did accomplish one major effort which should contribute in the longer run to giving new impetus to economic development. This was the completion of the agrarian reform, which puts much of the land in the hands of peasants who are more likely than the old landlords to put it into intensive cultivation, and which may force the old landlords to cultivate the land remaining to them in a much more technical way than they have traditionally done.

The Chilean case is a good example of the kind of pressures and crises with which a country is faced once the possibilities of import substitution have been largely exhausted. The intensification of inflation during the 1950s and thereafter, the stagnation of the economy for almost two decades, the social tensions which contributed much to the Allende victory in 1970, are all aspects of the post-import substitution crisis in that country. A failure to deal in time with this crisis was a major element leading to the tragedy which Chile has experienced since September 1973.

The Brazilian Post-Import Substitution Crisis

Brazil is a country with much vaster resources and a much larger population than Chile. However, even Brazil reached the end of import substitution possibilities by the early 1960s.

Efforts to industrialize Brazil were undertaken as early as the 1850s, and by the end of World War One there was an extensive textile industry in the country. In the 1920s the government adopted protectionist policies. However, it was the Great Depression and the Revolution of 1930 which put Brazil definitely on the road to import substitution development. The 1930 uprising put Getulio Vargas in power. He was strongly in favor of industrialization, adopted protectionist policies, and used the resources of the Banco do Brasil to finance new manufacturing enterprises. He also adopted a policy of deliberately leaving alone the rural economy and the still potent large landowning class, while submitting the urban working class to extensive control by the state.

During the period in which Getulio Vargas remained in power (1930–1945), the industrialization of Brazil resulted in the establishment of industries producing most light consumer goods, such as textiles, shoes, and processed foodstuffs; a beginning was made in the iron and steel industry with the establishment of the government's Volta Redonda plant. In the next decade the import substitution process moved on to undertake production of heavier consumer goods such as radios, television sets, washing machines, etc. Finally, during the administration of President Juscelino Kubitschek (1956–1960), the Brazilian import substitution economic development moved into the last stage, with the establishment of the automobile, shipbuilding, and machine-tool branches of the economy, and marked expansion of steel and other heavy industries.

However, by the end of the Kubitschek administration, Brazil had virtually exhausted the possibilities of import substitution as a motor force for development. Thereafter, if Brazilian economic development was to continue, it would have to do so on the basis of the expansion of the market, either internally or in foreign trade.

Brazil experienced a crisis during the 1960s, during which the constitutional democratic system was destroyed, largely as a result of the inability of the Brazilian political system to bring about the economic, social, and political reforms which were necessary for the process of economic development to continue. Although President Janio Quadros, who succeeded Juscelino Kubitschek, came to power on the basis of a program of basic reform, he resigned when he encountered the first serious opposition to his program. His successor, João Goulart, also an advocate of reform, was overthrown, largely as a result of his incompetence and his attempts to govern by dividing all his potential opponents.

The four military regimes which have succeeded Goulart,

who was overthrown in April 1964, have carried out a number of the changes which were necessary if Brazilian economic development was to continue through the process of expanding the available market. These include a reorganization of the capital market, marked stimulus to agricultural expansion, vast increases in education, and the beginning of a serious program of domestic research and development. They also include the channeling of major resources into the development of some of the relatively underdeveloped parts of the nation, particularly the Northeast and Amazonian regions, and a major impetus to the development of overseas markets for some of Brazil's consumer goods industries.

The military regimes, however, have not undertaken in a serious way one of the most crucial reforms, the redistribution of land. Nor have they basically altered the tax system, to make it less regressive, although they have enforced the actual collection of taxes, particularly income taxes to a degree previously unknown.

In Brazil, as in Chile, the post-import substitution crisis contributed substantially to a breakdown of the constitutional democratic political system which had existed during the latter phases of the import substitution period. Thus the country has paid heavily in human and political terms for the partial resolution of this crisis which has occurred since the middle of the 1960s.

The Mexican Case

Mexico presents an example of a country in which the general limitations of the import substitution strategy of economic development as described in this book have not been fully applicable. As a result of the Mexican Revolution, which began in 1910, the country experienced the process of agrarian reform several decades before import-substitution industrialization was well started. This uprising, which began as a purely political insurrection against the dictatorship of Porfirio Díaz, became an insurrection of the peasants, and paved the way for the beginning of the legal redistribution of much of the country's agricultural holdings in the 1920s and 1930s. By the time the serious process of import substitution had begun in the early 1940s, at least half of the cultivated land of Mexico had been placed in the hands of the beneficiaries of the agrarian reform.

As a result of the agrarian reform, a large part of the rural population which had not been in the market previously was made part of the market for at least some of the goods produced by the factories which were established through import substitution. In addition, the former large landlords, who were left with reduced holdings, were forced by the agrarian reform to transform themselves into economically progressive farmers in order to maintain their levels of income and living. Largely as a result of this, Mexican agriculture experienced a spectacular increase in output and productivity. Throughout the 1940s, 1950s, and 1960s it was able to more than keep ahead of the increase in Mexico's population (one of the world's most rapid) and to provide the populace with increasing amounts of food and the new industries with a large part of the raw materials they needed.

One other factor in the Mexican situation helped to prevent, or at least postpone, the kind of post-import substitution crisis as we have described as occurring in Chile and Brazil. This was the fact that during the import substitution phase, Mexico developed several new sources of income. The most important of these was tourism, which by the late 1960s was bringing almost a billion dollars a year into the economy. A second was sugar, which grew rapidly and became a major export during the 1960s, when Mexico received part of the United States sugar quota which had formerly been held by Cuba. Finally, partly as a result of her participation in the Latin American Free Trade Area, Mexico had begun by the late 1960s to export appreciable quantities of manufactured goods to other parts of the hemisphere and substantial amounts of semiprocessed goods and even some manufactured goods to the United States.

Mexico's import substitution industrialization moved apace in the three decades following 1940. It covered not only such fields of light consumer goods as textiles, shoes, and processed foods, but also heavier consumer goods such as household appliances, construction materials, and iron and steel and petro-chemicals, and finally such products as automobiles and machine tools. By the late 1960s Mexico rated with Brazil as one of the two Latin American countries with the most integrated industrial sectors.[1]

However, even Mexico would perhaps not be totally immune from the post-import substitution problem. By the early 1970s the government of President Luis Echeverría had launched a number of programs which indicated that he realized the possibility of such a problem. These included measures to spur substantially more resources into the development of agriculture, programs for encouraging the development of the relatively backward areas of the southern part of the republic, and measures to bring about higher returns for the lower-income elements of the nations's cities.

The Echeverría government's policies have aroused a degree of opposition from powerfully entrenched economic interests, which is unusual in the recent history of Mexico. Industrialists and other elements have publicly attacked the government, and even the president, in a way which indicated a possible breakdown in the wide degree of consensus which has marked Mexican political life since the late 1930s. Such a breakdown might provoke a degree of political turbulence and unrest which might well provoke a reentry of the military (which as an institution has been out of politics since the early 1940s) into active political participation, imperiling the regime and offering a serious handicap to the process of economic development.

The Venezuelan Case

Venezuela, like Mexico, has not faced the same kind of post-import substitution crisis as did Chile and Brazil, because it accompanied import substitution with basic social changes. However, it is a good example of the limitations of import substitution imposed upon many countries because of the relatively small size of its population. At the same time, it is an untypical case because of the vast resources which are provided by the nation's oil export industry.

Beginning in 1959, Venezuela underwent a deliberate and rapid policy of import substitution industrialization. Substantial resources drawn from oil exports were ploughed into the stimulation of manufacturing, particularly through the government's Venezuelan Development Corporation and Industrial Bank, while at the same time extensive protectionism was practiced not only through tariff policy but through a system of quotas and embargoes on imports.

While import substitution industrialization was an avowed governmental policy, important reforms were also being carried on. In the fifteen years following 1959, a large portion of the country's accessible cultivatable land was transferred from large landowners to small cultivators. Substantial sums were also expended on providing new peasant proprietors with credit, technical assistance, and help in marketing as well as with schools, medical facilities, potable water supplies, and electricity. Unlike most other countries, as a result, Venezuela saw a marked increase in agricultural output accompaning import substitution industrialization and agrarian reform.

However, by the early 1970s Venezuela was approaching the end of the import substitution process serving as the main force for further development. This was because the country has only some ten million people. Even if all of these are brought into the market, this is too small a base for a thoroughly integrated industrial economy. As a result, Venezuela finds itself under particular pressure to look abroad for new markets.

As one aspect of this search for foreign markets, Venezuela has joined the Andean Group. The government's basic hope, however, is that the country can exploit its very substantial natural endowment to become a significant supplier of the products of heavy industry, as well as nontraditional agricultural products.

The Venezuelan problem of finding possibilities for pushing development beyond the import substitution phase is greatly alleviated by its large petroleum output. The oil price increases of 1973–1974, which give some indications of being largely maintained for some years into the future, give added value to the country's petroleum reserves.

The Venezuelans are planning to use these resources to bring about basic and rapid transformation in their economy. A hitherto long-range program for expanding steel production from 1 million tons to 10 million tons is now made feasible as a relatively short-run effort, which can be fulfilled in the time it takes physically to plan for and expand the steel industry's facilities. When this program is completed, all the country's iron exports will be in the form of processed or at least semiprocessed iron and steel products. Similarly, vast programs for augmenting the output of the nation's petrochemical industry on a long-term basis seem likely to be executed in a relatively short span of years. Officials of the Venezuelan steel and petrochemical industries report that they have backlogs of orders from abroad which will easily keep their expanded enterprises busy for the foreseeable future.

At the same time, a substantial portion of the augmented petroleum export income will be poured into a massive expansion of Venezuelan agriculture. Not only will a policy of import substitution for agricultural products be carried out, but there is hope that a wide range of new exports of agricultural products, many of them in a processed or semiprocessed form, can be launched.

Thus Venezuela, like the other three countries which have used import substitution that we have discussed, underscores the fact that import substitution is but one phase in the process of development during the import substitution period, but it also underscores the need for a new strategy of economic development once the possibilities of import substitution have been exhausted. Furthermore, unlike Mexico and Brazil, Venezuela illustrates a case in which the post-import substitution strategy must be based largely on expanding the foreign market for the country's products rather than on the expansion of the internal market, the possibilities of which are severely limited by the nations's small population.

Conclusion

These capsulized case studies of several Latin American countries present a number of instances in Latin America in which the import substitution strategy of development has been used. They indicate perhaps that no nation has followed or is likely to follow exactly the model of this process which we have presented in this book. However, hopefully, they also indicate how in a few nations of the Western Hemisphere the general lines of the process which we have described have been applicable. Finally, they give some indication of the kind of development paths likely to be followed by less advanced nations elsewhere in Latin America as well as in Africa and Asia.

NOTES

1. For further information on Mexican industrialization, see Sanford Mosk's *Industrial Revolution in Mexico* (Berkeley: University of California Press, 1950); Frank Tannenbaum's *Mexico: The Struggle for Peace and Bread* (New York: Knopf, 1950); and Raymond Vernon's *The Dilemma of Mexican Development* (Cambridge, Mass.: Harvard University Press, 1963).

Postscript

A theoretical framework such as the one presented in this book, if it is to be worth anything, should be able to answer certain questions, and thus make easier the understanding of certain aspects of the problem with which it deals. It should also be defensible against certain kinds of criticisms which are likely to be raised against it. These last few pages will be devoted to looking at a few such questions which are perhaps answered by what has gone before, and to answering some objections which we suspect will be made to what we have said.

The first question concerning economic development to which we think we have at least provided part of the answer is that which is sometimes stated more as a charge than as an interrogation: How is it possible for there to be what appears to be substantial industrialization without this apparently changing the traditional society and economy, particularly in the rural segment of the country involved? This question is often followed by a denial of the "reality" of industrialization and economic development which has occurred on the grounds that it has left the traditional economy and society intact.

We feel that an understanding of the implications of the import substitution strategy of development provides an answer to these issues. There is no need for a confrontation between the new industrialized sector of the economy and the traditional rural sector during import substitution because the industrial segment is not seriously hampered in its development by the backward nature of the traditional society, and the traditional society is only tangentially affected by the industrialization process during the import substitution·phase.

In the first place, the market upon which the new industries depend for their development during the import substitution phase is almost completely urban. Second, industries will not be set up in this process until the market already established by imports has passed what Albert Hirschman calls "the domestic production threshold," that is, a size large enough to justify the establishment of one or more plants to produce the goods in question. Hence, during the import substitution phase, when the industrialization problem is largely a "physical" one of assembling the plant, equipment, labor force, management, and technical staff necessary to turn out the formerly imported goods, the fact that retrograde traditional agriculture keeps much of the population out of the market and doesn't provide adequate foodstuffs and raw materials is not a serious impediment to the continuance of industrialization. As a result, the industrialists and political leaders associated with them feel no great impulse to challenge the entrenched positions of those who dominated the traditional society.

On the other hand, the traditional rural ruling class is only modestly inconvenienced by the rise of industrialism in the cities during this phase. They can remain virtually sovereign within their own sphere. They might prefer foreign-made goods to the products of the new national industries. However, they will probably do little more than grumble about the higher prices and poorer quality of the domestic products, or if they really insist, will pay considerably higher prices to continue to import the foreign ones. The labor of which the rural landlords are deprived because it is attracted to the cities in part as a result of industrialization is marginal, and is usually more than offset by high rates of population increase in the rural areas.

Thus, during the import substitution phase of development, there is little direct cause for an all-out confrontation between the new society and economy based on industry and the old one based on traditional agriculture—a confrontation which would be very expensive for both sides. The industrialists haven't the immediate incentive to launch such a struggle, and probably wouldn't have the political power necessary to be successful in it until the import substitution process has made considerable headway. The landlords, so long as they are left alone in their own domain, will be content to preserve what they have and will generally look down upon the industrialists as social parvenus, except when they allow their daughter to marry the son of a manufacturer, thus enriching both the diluted family blood strain and their offspring's patrimony.

A second major question concerning economic development has been answered, we believe, by the analysis in the present volume. This is a question which has been raised, with a tone of hurt surprise in recent years, in publications of the Economic Commission for Latin America, one of the great protagonists during the 1940s and 1950s of the import substitution strategy: Why doesn't import substitution generate a self-sustaining process of development and growth?

We have demonstrated, we believe, that this question is based on a misunderstanding of the import substitution process. Import substitution is a phase of economic development; it is a way of getting industrialization well started, but it is not a guarantee that this process will carry a nation forward to a fully integrated economy in which all of the populace is in the market and the motor force of the economy is stimulation of the mass market.

A country which has used the import substitution strategy as we have described it will inevitably reach a stage at which import substitution ceases to be the motor force for development. Unless, at that point, it more or less consciously turns from the process of building enterprises to produce goods for a market already established by imports, to the process of expanding the existing market, such a country will be sure to find itself faced with stagnation. Yet, as we have also pointed out, such a switch in national economic objectives involves a severe economic, social, and political crisis. The ability of a country to overcome such a crisis will depend upon whether the balance of political power has shifted sufficiently as the result of the import substitution experience to permit a successful challenge to the traditional ruling class and upon the ability of the national leaders to see clearly the nature of the problem facing them.

However, the fact that the import substitution strategy of development has certain natural limits beyond which it is not useful is not an adequate basis for the argument that it should not be used at all. Of the possible strategies for development, import substitution is the most readily available, and probably the least painful, in terms of the living standards of the people of the developing country and probably in terms of political freedom.

A third question concerning economic development which receives at least a partial answer from a study of the import substitution strategy is the one asked even by some economists who tend to favor the strategy: Why do the developing countries generally opt for "unbalanced development"? Otherwise stated, this might be asked, why do the developing countries tend so persistently to interpret "economic development" as meaning industrialization?

The advocates of balanced growth argue that unless there is all-around development, of agriculture as well as a wide range of industries simultaneously, no single industry is apt to find a sufficient market for its products. However, as our analysis demonstrates, import substitution is not the first, but rather the second, phase of a nation's development. To a certain degree, markets for manufactured goods have been established as a result of the growth of a basisc export industry, usually a raw material or foodstuff, and until the import substitution process begins, the demand for these goods is met by imports. Furthermore, a new manufacturing plant is not likely to be established until the quantity of imports indicates that the market is sufficient to justify its installation. In addition, the strategy tends to expand markets, both by bringing new groups into the money economy and by creating a demand for the raw materials, machinery, and other inputs used by the first industries established through the process of import substitution.

Finally, an analysis of the import substitution strategy and its implications indicates that the concentration on industry is not likely to be permanent. Not only has it been preceded by a period during which emphasis was on the growth either of mining or agriculture, but if economic development is to continue, the import substitution phase must be succeeded by one in which considerable concentration must be placed upon agriculture.[1]

Indeed, "import substitution" is in some ways the wrong phase for the process which generally goes under this name, and which we used throughout this book. In fact, the real process of import substitution will in all likelihood continue after the substitution of manufactured goods has been more or less completed; but agricultural products, raw materials, and semiprocessed components will take the place of manufactured goods as the products for which substitutes will be produced domestically.

A fourth issue which is sometimes raised with regard to economic development and its political implications may also be explained by an understanding of the import substitution process. This is the question of why the industrialists in deveveloping countries, as a class, generally have little enthusiasm for a land redistribution program. It is often presumed that there is a conflict of interest between the industrialist and the traditional landowner because the persistence of the traditional landholding system limits the size of the market for the industrialists' products. Therefore, it is supposed, the industrialists should in their own interest be inclined to favor a redistribution of the land, which will put it in the hands of those who cultivate it, who will thus become recipients of a money income they didn't receive before (and hence, customers for industry). At the same time, hopefully, the new landowners will be more inclined to make efficient use of the land, growing a larger quantity of the agricultural products needed by the urban centers of industry.

Some of those who have observed this situation and noted a lack of enthusiasm on the part of the industrialists for land reform, find as an explanation a supposed desire on the industrialists' part to "assimilate" to the older landed aristocracy, and even to become landholders of the traditional type themselves. Although in individual cases this kind of motivation is not to be discounted completely, it is not an adequate or even very satisfactory explanation of the industrialists' general lack of enthusiasm for agrarian reform.

A much more adequate explanation is that during the import substitution phase there is not, in fact, any substantial conflict of interest between the industrialists and the traditional landlords. So long as the industrialists can develop and expand their enterprises by meeting the demand of a market which already exists, their progress is not impeded by the large landholding system and its maintenance of a substantial part of the rural population outside of the money economy. Only in the post-import substitution period does such a conflict arise. And it is perhaps not a surprise, therefore, to find that in countries such as Chile, Venezuela, or Peru, which have either entered or are approaching the post-import substitution phase of economic development, there is little objection to—and in fact some sentiment in favor of—agrarian reform on the part of the industrialists.

Finally, questions which have arisen over the role of labor in the industrialization process in currently developing countries can be explained by adequate understanding of import substitution. The existence of trade unionism and of extensive social and labor legislation in the developing countries has been widely noticed and has given rise to at least two different types of observations which are both generally mistaken.

One typical reaction to this phenomenon is that offered by Clark Kerr, John Dunlop, Frederick Harbison, and Charles Meyers in their well-known book *Industrialism and Industrial Man*. They comment with regard to the developing countries that: "as a result of the conventions and resolutions of the ILO and the demonstration effect of highly industrialized societies, they adopt elaborate systems of social security for their industrial working forces. In some cases . . . they move too far and too fast in this direction by instituting measures which are too costly for their stage of development. . . ."[2]

Other observers, particularly those of the more radical left, assert that the industrial workers in the developing countries are a "labor aristocracy," and in the process of acquiring this status have "sold their birthright." Typical of this approach is the following comment by Carlos Romero:

> This structure makes it possible for the major industrial concerns to earn enormous profits and pay wages and salaries considerably higher than the national average. Also, copying the techniques of the big American companies, they offer all manner of material advantages and assistance to their workers and employees. They build towns for the use of their personnel, subsidize popular dining rooms, amusement parks, sports fields, etc. The company ties its workers to it and also separates them from their natively employed fellow workers by the differential in living standards and job security.[3]

An understanding of the import substitution process gives a better explanation than either of these for the position of labor in the developing countries. The fact is that, with a more or less assured market during the import substitution phase for what they can produce, industrialists are willing to pay the higher labor costs which are involved in dealing with unions, obeying labor and social laws, and providing various

kinds of benefits which are unusual in the highly industrialized nations. Also, for the same reason, governments
are not loath to submit to political pressures for labor and
social legislation and the legalization of unions and collective
bargaining.

Because the expansion of the market is not a significant
problem during the import substitution period, the increased
labor and social costs of industrialists, noted by the two
books we have just quoted, do not hamper the expansion of
industrialization during that period. Furthermore, the provision of more adequate wages and better working and living
conditions for industrial workers helps to solve one of the
"physical" problems of development during import substitution which we have noted previously: to assemble a
stable and sufficiently efficient work force to be able to
produce the manufactured goods for which the readily available market is calling.

This process does not necessarily involve any "betrayal"
or "selling of their birthright" by the industrial workers
involved. Rather, it means that, because of the strategy of
import substitution, these workers are able to get for themselves a somewhat higher proportion of the return from the
increase in their productivity (resulting from being transferred from subsistence agriculture to manufacturing employment) than might otherwise be possible. Indeed, a good
case could be made for the argument that one of the principal
virtues of the import substitution strategy of development is
that it forces the new industrial workers to pay a much
smaller part of the real costs of development than do alternative strategies.

At least two criticisms which may possibly be made
against our analysis are worthy of comment. The first concerns our method of theorizing. For more than two decades
we have observed how economic development has in fact
been taking place in various parts of the world, particularly

in Latin America. From these observations, we have sought in the present book to generalize, to try to develop a model which would explain most aspects of how this process has been going forward.

Judging from the reception given to some other books on economic problems appearing in recent years which have sought to theorize on more or less this same basis, we are aware that there are those who believe that we have begun from the wrong starting point in seeking to develop a theory concerning economic development. They would argue that instead of studying the facts of a problem and attempting to put them in some reasonable order, theorizing should commence with the objective to be obtained, in this case economic development, and through the application of logical reasoning, one step after the other should be taken to ascertain how the objective should be reached.

There are perhaps two answers which can be made to such an argument. The first is that the theory we have presented about the import substitution strategy of development seems to answer most pertinent questions which have been raised about it. The second is that in theorizing as we have done, we are in good company. Although we have no intention of comparing our achievements with theirs, we would argue that Adam Smith drew his basic theories largely from his observations of the way in which the mercantilist system was operating, and that economic development was progressing in eighteenth century Britain; that David Ricardo evolved his theory of rent largely from his analysis of the practical effects of the functioning of the Corn Laws; and that even John Maynard Keynes developed his theories of the cause and cure of economic instability from his extensive analyses of the depressed state of the economy of post-World War One Great Britain.

A second criticism is one which has been offered by a colleague upon reading an early draft of our discussion of import substitution development. This colleague argued that all the writer was doing was presenting a defense for inefficiency.

It seems to us that this argument distorts what we have attempted to do in the present book. We start out with the proposition that except for unusual cases new industries in developing countries are almost certain to be inefficient when compared to similar industries in the already developed nations, for reasons which we have noted. What we have done is not to excuse this—it is not something which needs to be either defended, excused, or condemned—but rather to indicate why it is possible for industrialization and general economic development to proceed for a considerable distance in spite of this inefficiency. Our argument also indicates the limit beyond which inefficiency becomes a serious drawback to further economic development.

To sum up, we have tried to present a detailed analysis of the most commonly used method by which underdeveloped nations are attempting to industrialize at the present time and to investigate the implications of this method. If we have succeeded in making the process of economic development more comprehensible, this book will have been of use to all those who are concerned about a most important problem.

NOTES

1. We agree completely with Albert Hirschman's arguments that a country is not likely to have sufficient resources to develop all aspects of its economy at the same time, and that unbalanced development provides many opportunities for induced investment decisions. Our analysis of import substitution merely reinforces the reasoning of Hirschman.

2. Clark Kerr, John Dunlop, Frederick Harbison, and Charles Meyers, *Industrialism and Industrial Man* (Cambridge: Harvard University Press, 1960), p. 181.

3. Carlos Romero, "Revolutionary Practice and Theory in Latin America," in Irving Louis Horowitz, Josue de Castro, and John Gerassi, eds., *Latin American Radicalism* (New York: Random House, 1969), p. 581.

BIBLIOGRAPHICAL NOTE

The bibliography available on the general question of economic development is voluminous. Unfortunately, much of it contains at best only tangential reference to the strategy of import substitution. Rather than present here a huge list of the writings available generally on economic development, we will confine ourselves to listing only those works to which we have referred directly or have quoted in the preceding pages.

Alexander, Robert J. *Agrarian Reform in Latin America.* New York: Macmillan, 1974.

————. *A Primer of Economic Development.* New York: Macmillan, 1962.

————. *Labor Relations in Argentina, Brazil and Chile.* New York: McGraw-Hill, 1962.

Bauer, P.J. *Economic Analysis and Policy in Underdeveloped Countries.* Durham, N.C.: Duke University Press, 1957.

Economic Commission for Latin America. *La cooperatión internacional en la politica de desarrollo latinoamericano.* New York: United Nations, 1954.

————. *The Process of Industrial Development in Latin America.* New York: United Nations, 1966.

Enke, Stephen. *Economics for Development.* Englewood Cliffs, N.J.: Prentice-Hall, 1963.

Hagen, Everett. *The Economics of Development.* Homewood, Ill.: Richard E. Irwin, 1968.

Hirschman, Albert O. *The Strategy of Economic Development.* New Haven: Yale University Press, 1958.

Horowitz, Irwin Louis; Castro, Josue de; and Gerassi, John, eds. *Latin American Radicalism: A Documentary Report on Left and Nationalist Movements.* New York: Random House. 1969.

167

Krause, Walter, *International Economics*. Boston: Houghton Mifflin, 1965.

Lewis, W. Arthur. *Development Planning: The Essentials of Economic Policy*. New York: Harper & Row, 1968.

————. and Baldwin, Robert E. *Economic Development: Theory, History, Policy*. New York: John Wiley & Sons, 1957.

Mosk, Sanford. *Industrial Revolution in Mexico*. Berkeley: University of California Press, 1950.

Myrdal, Gunnar. *An International Economy: Problems and Prospects*. New York: Harper & Brothers, 1956.

Nurkse, Ragnar. *Problems of Capital Formation in Underdeveloped Countries and Patterns of Trade and Development*. New York: Oxford University Press, 1967.

Prebisch, Raul. *The Economic Development of Latin America and Its Principal Problems*. Lake Success, N.Y.: United Nations, 1950.

————. *Towards a Dynamic Development Policy for Latin America*. New York: United Nations, 1963.

————. *Transformación y desarrollo: La gran tarea de la América Latina*. Mexico: Fondo de Cultura Económica, 1970.

Proceedings of the United Nations Conference on Trade and Development, Volume IV: Trade in Manufacture. New York: United Nations, 1964.

Sokoloff, Joe. *The Import Substitution Strategy of Economic Development, The Chilean Case*. Ph.D diss., Rutgers University, 1974.

Tannenbaum, Frank. *Mexico: The Struggle for Peace and Bread*. New York: Knopf, 1950.

Tavares, Maria Concepção. "Auge y declinación del proceso de sustitución de importaciones en el Brasil," *Boletin Económico de América Latina,* vol. 1, no. 1 (March 1964).

Theberge, James D., ed. *Economics of Trade and Development*. New York: John Wiley & Sons 1968. (Especially article by Harry G. Johnson: "Tariffs and Economic Development," reprinted from *The Journal of Development Studies,* vol. 1, no. 1, October 1964).

Vernon, Raymond. *The Dilemma of Mexican Development*. Cambridge: Harvard University Press, 1963.

Williamson, Harold F. and Buttrick, John A., eds. *Economic Development: Principles and Patterns*. New York: Prentice-Hall, 1954.